CULINARY TRAVELS

Memories Made at the Table

Emily Szajda

Black Rose Writing | Texas

Second printing

ISBN: 978-1-68513-074-9
PUBLISHED BY BLACK ROSE WRITING
www.blackrosewriting.com

Printed in the United States of America
Suggested Retail Price (SRP) $45.95

Culinary Travels is printed in Goudy Old Style

*As a planet-friendly publisher, Black Rose Writing does its best to eliminate unnecessary waste to reduce paper usage and energy costs, while never compromising the reading experience. As a result, the final word count vs. page count may not meet common expectations.

Dedication

To my mother-in-law, Teresa Szajda, for sharing her passion for the Polish kitchen with me and being an unwavering support. My Grandma Barb for taking my hand as a child and ushering me up to the stovetop. And to my cherished children and ever-hungry husband--thank you for your patience, your astute taste, and your unabashed want for more.

And finally, to all those I have met on my travels near and far, you have left me with everlasting memories of a life well lived. Cheers!

Teściowej Teresie Szajdzie za podzielenie się ze mną pasją do polskiej kuchni i nieustanne wsparcie. Mojej Babci Barbarze za wzięcie mnie za rękę w dzieciństwie i zaprowadzenie do kuchni. A moim ukochanym dzieciom i wiecznie głodnemu mężowi dziękuję za cierpliwość, oryginalny smak i niepohamowane pragnienie więcej.

I wreszcie wszystkim tym, których spotkałam podczas moich bliskich i dalekich podróży: zostawiliście mnie ze wspomnieniami dobrze przeżytego życia. Wasze zdrowie!

CULINARY TRAVELS

Memories Made at the Table

TABLE OF CONTENTS

Prologue | The Travel Bug

Food is life, a portrayal of our human experience, provoking conversation, and intimacy with those you share it with and the environment around us.

Months of preparations and the time had finally come. Meeting in Gdańsk, my family flew in from the United States, namely my father, brother, and grandmother, to meet my friends from across the European continent for an international wedding celebration. An amalgamation of cultures and backgrounds, my husband's family being in the majority in his hometown, gathered on the rooftop terrace of the stylish Marina Club Hotel overlooking the historic old town of Gdańsk.

Most old cities in Europe are architectural gems, and Gdańsk is no different. It was decimated in World War II and restored to its medieval splendor. The tall standing buildings painted in a splash of vibrant hues accentuate the Dutch influence in the city. It made for the picture-perfect backdrop to an unforgettable moment in time.

In a salute, we raised glasses of Spanish cava to the sky thanking our family and friends who had traveled great lengths to commemorate our union. Six months to the day before this, we said our "I do's" in a lawyer's office in a small civil service in Marengo, Iowa. Followed by an intimate celebration at a friend's wine bar, both events serve as tiny snapshots in time I have collected in my treasure trove I consider my memory. From toasted bruschetta and artisan pizza to the most decadent vanilla, lemon, and blackberry impromptu wedding cake hosted by Solera to the herbed venison and buttery poached Baltic cod served as the mains at our chef-prepared four-course dinner catered by

Szafarnia 10, the food was important to me and reflected our taste and journey together.

Memories. Photographic images tucked away in the catalog of the mind.

When I set the intention of writing a cookbook, this the first of many to come, I thought about the wealth of food experiences I have had throughout my life. Recollections from Christmases long ago, my Great Aunt Darlene preparing buttery sweet rolls from scratch and using the pan drippings from the turkey to make gravy, slathering butter on a slice of fresh-baked sourdough, eating clam chowder from a styrofoam cup on Fisherman's Wharf in San Francisco. We capture the sensory richness, taste, smell, and texture of the foods we eat in our episodic memory. This catalog files the personal, unique, and concrete experiences we can retrieve from our past. Setting the stage, this time capsule lays the foundation for this cookbook.

Sitting at a sun-drenched picnic table in the side yard of a Croatian home, eating freshly shucked oysters and sipping their yearly batch of crisp white wine, episodic memories differ from semantic memory in that the latter is autobiographic. The difference lies between the reminiscing often triggered by a sensation (sight, sound, taste, touch, or smell) and knowing a fact. For example, London is the capital of England, or how to do something, i.e., tie our shoes. Distinguishing the two, Endel Tulving, psychologist and cognitive neuroscientist at the University of Toronto, realized the dissimilarity in 1972. This tidbit of historical knowledge went straight into your semantic memory; how chance is that?

This book will focus on our episodic memory associated with new experiences, conversations, relationships with others and of place, and breaking down barriers to foster understanding and community. It sounds like a big ambition, but the simple act of pulling up a chair at a table and "breaking bread" can ignite a profound consciousness that can be revolutionary to how we experience and engage in the world around us. Food is not merely sustenance but life-in-action, in *memory*, in love, and in abundance if only we open our eyes to see it this way.

Food is life-giving. It provides us with the energy to show up every day and plays a significant factor in supporting a healthy diet and lifestyle. It also acts as a representation of who we are. Food is a creative art form, a culmination of self-expression and one's life experiences to be consumed by others. A ripple poured out into another, then another.

Having traveled extensively and resided in Europe, I can say that I made my fondest memories and friendships abroad in the kitchen and around the table. Individuals from across the globe join together to satisfy a basic human need but reap a benefit so much greater. Living in a period mired in polarity and divisiveness, I believe we can foster cultural empathy through understanding and relationship-building. We must share ourselves for others to know the intricacies, the fibers that make up our whole self, and not just some glossed-over stereotype that only scrapes the surface and incites assumptions. Backpacking through Europe, which inspired my flight from the familiarities of home and move abroad, instilled in me a curious hunger to learn more. Meeting strangers, locals, and ex-pats alike, I found that we had more in common than one might think.

The human experience. Whether sipping a coffee with a friend I met in a youth hostel after the Color Run in Cologne or a chance encounter with a musician on a train bound for Prague where I was invited to dinner meeting his friends, a group of eclectic individuals, at a local Bohemian restaurant I would never have stumbled upon, I have found the most exciting conversations ultimately arise when inhibitions are quelled, walls fall, and everyone feels at ease to join the conversation.

After a decade or more of traversing borders through Europe, I want to share the recipes that captivated my palate and the savory moments that left me wanting more. I found my passion and purpose in conversations and chance meetings. I slowed down life to see the intricacies that made it even fuller. Who knew food had such clout, teaching us how to engage in life?

Open your heart and mind. Learn how my cooking style is influenced by my travels, a fusion of taste, flavor, technique, and preference. Did you know, for instance, that coffee companies like Nespresso create different consumer profiles for other countries based on the general archetype of the nation? Pastries in Europe are often less sweet than those concocted in the United States. And some regions of France are known for using butter. In contrast, others use lard or olive oil based on their geographical location and production of said fat.

Without further ado, whet your appetite, and pull up a chair as I take you on a culinary tour across Europe sharing my renditions of the much-loved fare that defines the gastronomy of nations and the memories made along the way.

Germany, Austria, & Switzerland | Ancestry & Community
Multisensory Experiences Conjure up the Greatest Memories

Changing the trajectory of my life, my high school German teacher, Frau Fredericks, opened a door I never knew existed. Traveling through Germany, Austria, and Switzerland the summer after graduation was a grand adventure for a girl only seventeen who had grown up in a small town in the heart of the Midwest. Simple and foundational. Softball games and Friday night lights defined the early part of my childhood. Family suppers gathered around the table consisted of traditional American fare meatloaf served with mashed potatoes with an occasional lima bean added color to the plate. We only felt cultural diversity when we dined in the Amana Colonies, a German settlement established in 1823, not but a short drive from home.

The close-knit community felt like the set of the 1980's television series Cheers, where everyone knew your name. Later in my adolescence, when my mother and father divorced, and my mom moved away, family life became vague, if not non-existent. I looked to my teachers and grandparents to help influence my future path.

My grandmothers would play a major role in fostering my relationship with food. Pulling up a stepstool to the stovetop was an often occurrence. From making homemade playdough to the nostalgic comfort food of chipped beef gravy on toast, both women on my mother and father's side passed down their family traditions to me.

Mired by the tragic September 11th attacks on the World Trade Center in New York City in 2001, Frau Frederick's biennial trip to Germany had been rescheduled for the summer after my high school graduation. While living in two different parts of the country, my parents rarely saw eye to eye, but they did agree on one thing: they did not want me to go. This opportunity posed the most decisive point in my young life and was in defiance of their wishes. Having been bitten by the travel bug, I knew that there would be no going back once I had a taste of Europe.

Germany, Austria, and Switzerland were dots on the roadmap across the continent. From eating cafeteria-style in youth hostels to dining in more rustic, family-owned restaurants tucked down charming medieval alleyways and villages that nestled in the valleys of the Alps, I felt engulfed by the culture, the heart, and soul of each country I visited.

I was never raised to be a culinarian. In fact, I was quite a picky eater, conditioned by generation after generation of heirloom recipes that got watered down over time.

Funding my travels, I had worked my way through high school at a truck stop diner serving tables and making liver and onions, among a host of not so flattering yet tasty midwestern dishes. It wasn't glamorous. Honestly, the food and beverage industry rarely is enchanting, but it did pay the bills and more. Not only would it send me packing along the Romantische Straße, a picturesque 350km route through the forests and mountains of

Bavaria and Baden-Württemberg in Southern Germany, but it would also allow me to study culinary arts and hospitality management. Luring me away from a career in interior design at Iowa State University, the culinary program at Kirkwood College offered global travel study programs in Jamaica, Italy, and Australia at the time. Tantalized by the prospect of submerging myself in Italy's history, allure, and opulence, I chose to study amongst the Florentines, touring the majestic towns along the Cinque Terre and throughout the countryside of Tuscany.

My trip to Germany would be the starting point; I would escape to Europe year after year until I finally made the leap and moved abroad in 2013.

From visiting Check Point Charlie and relaxing in the English-inspired Tiergarten in Berlin, enjoying a pint and pretzel at one of the many beer gardens the capital city boasts, that very first trip would take me from the North to the South, from Bavaria, across the border to Mozart's Salzburg, securing a ride on the Jungfrau Railway to walk on glaciers in Switzerland and back to the center of European banking, Frankfurt am Main.

Not knowing I would one day participate in the Color Run in Cologne or go on a romantic stroll through the gothic German town of Aachen along the Belgian border, where we would tuck into a delicatessen famed for its homemade Italian specialties two years later, I lived life in the moment through sensations. Every experience was new, and I felt lucky to be afforded such a gift.

Reminiscing now, I can still taste the pesto on my grilled panini and feel the sun on my shoulders as I sat for a strong coffee with a new friend I made after that famed run.

The essence of life is not found in materialistic things but in the happiness and memories fostered along the way. And while I never felt like it would be my last trip to any destination, I made it a point to be present. Undistracted by social media, to-dos, or places to be, I immersed myself in the multisensory experience.

From the raindrops clattering down on my umbrella as we raced from one portico across the square to that little delicatessen to smelling the fresh-baked rye bread and pickled onions at my host family's home in Würzburg as we sat for a cold picnic-style dinner, I have always been curious, like a child experiencing the world for the first time. If you want to create a lasting memory, make sure your senses are sparked and order something new you have never had before. Take your tastebuds on a trip. And when your dish arrives, digest the whole dining experience before indulging in that first bite.

Sitting down to dinner in Regensburg on my journey northwest from Munich to Frankfurt am Main, I was greeted by other patrons who were already seated at my table. Strangers yes. An unusual practice for Americans so accustomed to dining as a private affair. In Germany, Frau Fredericks had taught us to be prepared that a host may seat groups together who have never met, utilizing space and beckoning diners to get friendly. Traveling solo was not such an unusual surprise as this had become my preferred way to trot across the continent; I was the token American among a restaurant of locals. Unforgettable was an understatement when the eyes of other guests gaped wide as I was served a large ham hock with bread dumplings drizzled with pan drippings, a dish the size of my head. What they were thinking, I could only guess. Gluttony? The restaurant was alight with laughter, the pork falling off the bone, and the pillowy bread dumplings, one of my favorite comfort foods. I devoured the experience. Like a warm hug, the feelings of utter satisfaction at my night's food selection, I dug in.

If we want to capture memories and make our lives unforgettable, we must slow down and harness the power of presence and firsts. Unconsciously, we race through life, jetting into a fast-food drive-through and back out again. While guaranteed to peek your alertness, that quick Starbucks coffee has no lasting value in making a memory unless you were drinking it on a first date, or your favorite comedian was in line behind you. In our daily life, we must step outside the norm. It doesn't have to be big, paying $500 for a 10-course meal, but stepping outside the box a bit may help. Invite your friends over for drinks and pica-pica al fresco or dine with your loved one at a candlelit table. These unique experiences take the ordinary and make life more extraordinary.

Looking back on my adventures across Germany, the recipes take me down memory lane to my childhood dining in the Amana Colonies, tasting spätzle for the first time, or enjoying a warm slice of apple strudel topped with a dollop of fresh whipped cream on a square in Dresden's Alt Stadt as I awaited a tour to begin.

We can all stroll down memory lane by tuning into taste. From grandma's homemade bread pudding drizzled with whiskey sauce or a first encounter with the black licorice flavor of Jägermeister- the thought makes shivers race up my spine. When we close our eyes, we can transgress time and space to that safe feeling of home or that memory reminding us not to overly indulge. We have all experienced tastes, sounds, smells, sights, or a touch that sends us back, provokes a sentiment of the familiar, of freedom, of love, of joy.

Braised Red Cabbage

Cabbage sounds boring, but braised red cabbage is far from ordinary with the hint of vinegar and dash of spice. Sitting down for a ham hock in Regensburg or slicing schnitzel after an afternoon at Oktoberfest in Munich, this simple dish would catch my eye on any menu. I am a glutton for sweet and savory.

A staple in the German kitchen- its sweet yet tart demeanor is the perfect accompaniment to make your palette sing. This dish gets better with age. Let it sit for a day in the refrigerator and reheat gently. It will keep for up to five days covered in the refrigerator.

1 large red cabbage, 2 to 2 ½ pounds, quartered, cored, and cut crosswise in thin strips

2 tablespoons olive oil

1 small onion, thinly sliced

2 tart green apples, Granny Smith, for example

½ cup water

6-8 tablespoons balsamic vinegar

¼ teaspoon clove

¼ teaspoon nutmeg sea salt freshly ground black pepper, to taste

Directions

Prepare cabbage and cover with cold water while you ready the other ingredients. Heat the olive oil over medium heat in a large, lidded pot, and add the onion. Cook, stirring until just tender and starting to become transparent about 2-3 minutes. Add 3 tablespoons of good quality balsamic vinegar. Stir to combine and cook until mixture is golden. Add the apples and stir for 2-3 minutes more. Drain the cabbage and add it to the pot. Toss to coat and add the clove, nutmeg, 3 more tablespoons of balsamic vinegar, ½ cup of water, and salt, to taste. Stir. Cover the pot and cook over low heat for one hour, stirring from time to time. Add freshly ground pepper, taste and adjust salt. If you prefer it a bit tarter, drizzle in an additional tablespoon or two of balsamic vinegar.

Roasted Garlic Soup

A velvet cream soup of roasted garlic garnished with fresh parsley and toasted bread.

I fell in love with this soup before the first bite. You will too, but caveat- you must adore garlic. The aroma of oven-roasted cloves envelops you like a warm blanket on a cold winter's day. Visualize the snow-topped Alps in Bavaria near the towns of Füssen or Oberstdorf, and you will get the idea. Out of the norm, on a weekend interlude to the Alps, surrounded by picturesque views of some of Europe's grandest peaks, doing something I am not so good at but utterly fancy, snowboarding, the stage was set. Cozying up with a bowl of this soup was tantalizing. With every sense encapsulated, it was like fireworks at night.

That is what this book is about...associations, and wow, I have many. Maybe you do too? Explore the milestones and the everyday occurrences surrounding food and discover a new appreciation. Take a bite, sit back, let the warmth surround you, and fill your heart.

2 tablespoons olive oil

3 bulbs roasted garlic, approximately 30 cloves

1 medium white onion, chopped

1 medium yellow potato, peeled and cubed

1 shallot, sliced

2 stalks celery, chopped

4 cups chicken stock

1 teaspoon dried thyme

1 teaspoon dried oregano

1 teaspoon dried marjoram

¾ teaspoon sea salt

¼ teaspoon white pepper

1 cup Greek yogurt

½ lemon, juiced

1 tablespoon fresh parsley, chopped, optional

Toasted day-old bread, crouton garnish

Directions

Preheat the oven to 425°F. Cut the tops off 3 bulbs of garlic, places them in a small baking pan, and drizzle 1 tablespoon olive oil over the cloves. Roast for 30-35 minutes until the garlic starts to pop out of the bulbs. Set aside to cool.

In a large stockpot over medium-to-medium low heat, slowly sauté the onions and celery until soft. Add the potatoes and stir for 1 minute. Continue by pouring in the chicken stock, and add the thyme, oregano, marjoram, salt, and pepper. Peeling the roasted garlic from the bulb, add the cloves to the liquid, and bring to a simmer for 10 minutes or until the potatoes are tender.

Remove from the heat. Add the yogurt and squeezed lemon. Using an immersion blender puree the soup until smooth. Garnish with fresh parsley and top with toasted day-old bread.

Beet Salad with Fresh Fennel, Mandarins, and Goat Cheese

Beets are a common ingredient in many countries across central Europe. From Poland and the Czech Republic to Germany. Pickled or pureed, roasted or as a soup, they are versatile and add brilliant color to the plate.

This simple salad looks and tastes like summer but highlights winter fruits and vegetables. It's that one dish that, when it feels drab and dull outside, brightens your spirits because of the vibrant colors and unique marriage of not necessarily usual flavors. I am not sure about you, but even as a chef, I do not cook with fennel all that often, but when it does grace the table, it reminds me how fond I am of the delicate anise seed flavor and aroma. I love it. Served at one of my yoga retreats in the north of Spain in early 2015 as a part of a cooking class, everyone tried their hand at thinly slicing the fennel, not so easy without training or a mandolin, and arranging the salad as though it were to be served in a high-end restaurant. After sending out a survey to get feedback on the retreat, students were in unison asserting they ate too much delicious fare. Not such a bad problem to have.

Allowing the salad to sit with the dressing helps to develop the flavor.

2 fennel bulbs, sliced thin

4 mandarins, peeled and segmented

¼ cup minced parsley

1 tablespoon olive oil

1 lemon, juiced

2 mandarins, juiced

1 teaspoon Dijon mustard

1-2 teaspoons honey

½ teaspoon sea salt

¼ teaspoon freshly ground black pepper

4 roasted beets, quartered

4 ounces goat cheese, crumbled

Directions

In a large bowl, toss together fennel, mandarins, parsley, salt, and pepper. Using a small jar or bowl and whisk, combine the olive oil, lemon and mandarin juices, Dijon mustard, and honey. Put the top on the jar, shake or whisk in a bowl to combine. Pour dressing over the salad. Toss and let rest for 20-40 minutes before serving to allow the flavors to develop.

Spoon the fennel salad onto plates and arrange the beets and goat cheese on top before serving.

Hunter's Pork Chops

Breaded buttermilk pork chops in a gravy of pork drippings and mushrooms.

Funny, growing up in the American Midwest, you somehow become accustomed to high-end cuts of beef and pork. I remember being in a boutique restaurant in Barcelona that worked with farmers near Girona that raised grass-fed cows and pigs. And while the products were top quality, the cuts were customarily thin based on what the population accepted as the norm. The slightest amount of heat would make a steak well done versus in Iowa for example, a steak that is thick and well done is not usually the temperature of choice.

While in Germany, there is a fair share of lighter dishes, one often thinks of heavier comfort foods that define their cuisine.

Buy your preferred pork chop cut, but do note cooking times may vary based on the thickness of the meat.

4 pork chops

Salt and pepper

Buttermilk and flour for dredging

¼ cup olive oil for frying

4 tablespoons butter

3 tablespoons flour

1 cup whole milk

1-2 cloves garlic, minced

8 oz button mushrooms, sliced

1 teaspoon Dijon mustard

2 teaspoons sweet paprika

1 cup beef stock

Ground black pepper

Sea salt, to taste

Directions

Salt and pepper both sides of the pork chops. Pour the buttermilk in a shallow bowl. Scoop some flour on a large plate. Submerge each pork chop in the buttermilk to coat both sides and let the excess liquid drip off. Dredge the pork chops in the flour, coating both sides. Repeat the process one more time to thicken the amount of breading on the pork chops. Refrigerate the pork chops for at least 15 minutes.

Heat olive oil in a heavy skillet over medium-high heat. Add the pork chops and fry until golden brown, about 3-4 minutes on each side. Remove the pork chops and set aside. Drain the oil and add the butter to melt. Then add the flour and constantly whisk for 3-4 minutes or until the mixture is a rich, caramel brown. Continue to whisk in the milk, paprika, beef bouillon cubes, and black pepper until thoroughly blended. Bring the mixture to a simmer, continuing to whisk. Add the mushrooms and continue to simmer, occasionally stirring, for 3 minutes. Add salt and pepper to taste. Place the pork chops in the sauce, leaving the tops exposed. Cover, reduce the heat to low, and simmer for 10-15 minutes or until the pork chops' center are done with an internal temperature of 145°F. Position the pork chops on individual plates and spoon the sauce over them. Serve immediately.

Coachman's Beef Goulash

An Austrian favorite of tender cuts of beef in a thick gravy seasoned with paprika, this recipe is a nod to the traditional Hungarian dish.

Four, five, six in the morning, there was this charming little restaurant near Vienna's West train station that served up traditional Austrian cuisine until the wee hours before daybreak. Located near many of the most popular youth hostels in the city like the Wombats or Be Free, this was a destination for locals and tourists alike. Mesmerized by the city and surrounding wine region, I have been to the Austrian capital many times and always make a note to stop in. From their flädlesuppe (German pancake soup) to sturm, a young wine, essentially fermented grape juice, and their friendly staff that is accustomed to serving an international clientele, the place feels like you are stepping foot in grandma's kitchen.

2-pound pasture-raised beef, top round roast, stewing beef or shoulder

2 medium onions, sliced

3 tablespoons, sweet paprika powder

1 teaspoon smoked paprika powder

1 teaspoon balsamic vinegar

1 teaspoon Worcestershire sauce

¼ cup tomato paste

3 cloves garlic, minced

1 teaspoon ground coriander

1 teaspoon marjoram

2 bay leaves

½ teaspoon ground black pepper

2-3 teaspoons sea salt

5 tablespoons olive oil

Beef stock

Ingredients for serving:

Knödle (bread dumplings) recipe follows

Frankfurter sausage

4 eggs

Pickled gherkins

Directions

Trim the meat by removing the ligaments, but not the meat's gelatinous parts, which add body to the juices. Cut the beef into bite-sized cubes and roughly chop the onions.

Heat the olive oil in a large pot over medium-low heat, add onions and cook slowly, constantly stirring until they are transparent. Sprinkle the paprika over the onions, and quickly stir in the vinegar, Worcestershire, and tomato paste. Add the meat, stir briefly, then flavor with garlic, coriander, salt, pepper, and marjoram. Add beef stock until the meat is just covered, and simmer on low for around 2 to 2 ½ hours until meat is soft. Stir occasionally and add small amounts of stock as juice is reduced.

Once the meat is cooked, add more stock, and allow the juice to cook for a final 10-15 minutes. Taste and adjust the seasoning according to your preference.

To serve, boil the sausage with small slits cut down the length of the link. Fry the eggs sunny side up. Slice the gherkins and fan them. Serve one knödle in the center of the goulash on a large plate or bowl and arrange other garnishes nestled to its side.

Knödle

With a hint of sage, I give a nod to my American roots.

The quintessential bread dumpling. Yes, there are no low carb diets here. When you think comfort, this is essential. Paired with braised ham, as a side to goulash or simply in a chicken broth, knödle are that German equivalent to Thanksgiving dressing. Unstrap the belt and order a second.

I don't think I have ever eaten a bad one. Don't let boiling bread scare you. It is easier than you think.

1 baguette

1 tablespoon butter

½ medium onion, chopped fine

3 tablespoons parsley

1 cup hot milk

1 ½ teaspoon sea salt

½ teaspoon ground black pepper

½ teaspoon dried sage

2 eggs

Directions

Slice the dried baguette into small cubes and place them in a large bowl. Pour the hot milk over the bread, cover, and let sit for 20-30 minutes or until softened. Heat the butter in a small sauté pan and cook the onions just until transparent. Add the cooked onions to the bread mixture along with the eggs, parsley, salt, pepper, and sage. Knead the mixture together with your hands until very thoroughly combined, breaking up as many of the bread cubes as you can until it's a soft and chunky-smooth consistency. If the dough is too mushy, add breadcrumbs (not flour).

Wet your hands to prevent the dough from sticking and form knödel about 2-inches in diameter (they will expand slightly when cooked). Press the knödel between your palms to make sure they're nice and compact. Bring a large, wide pot of salted water to a very light simmer with fizzy bubbles floating to the surface, but do not boil. Gently spoon the knödel in the water one at a time and let them "steep" 15-20 minutes. Do not at any point let the water boil or you risk your knödel crumbling.

Carefully lift them out with a slotted spoon.

Filet of Wild Trout with Forest Mushrooms

**A light pan-fried filet of trout is elevated by the earthy flavors of wild mushrooms and rosemary.
Fit for a restaurant, invite your friends, and serve up a glass of buttery chardonnay.**

Dishing up a memory that my Grandpa Larry would have adored, he was a man known for his fishing and camping. Transforming me into a tom girl, at least a fervent nature lover, was in part his influence. One of his signature dishes was a pepper dusted breaded catfish deep-fried. Whether staying the night at my grandparent's or camping at Lake Iowa, Grandpa could always whip up the day's catch on the fly. Years have passed, but the memory remains.

4-filets of trout

Flour for coating

Sea salt

Ground black pepper

1 lemon, juiced and zested

2 tablespoons olive oil

1 tablespoon butter

1-2 cloves garlic, minced

8 ounces specialty mushrooms (clamshell, shitake, trumpet royal, forest nameko, velvet pioppini)

Splash dry white wine

For the herb butter

5 tablespoons unsalted butter, room temperature

1-1 ½ teaspoon anchovy paste

1 teaspoon dried marjoram

1 teaspoon fresh rosemary

½ teaspoon dried oregano

½ lemon, juiced

2 tablespoons fresh parsley

Directions

Wash the fish fillets, pat dry, and season with salt and pepper. Drizzle with lemon juice and zest and set aside.

Finely chop the rosemary, combine it with the marjoram and oregano, and stir it in the butter. Season with salt, pepper, anchovy paste, and lemon juice. Set aside.

Clean and finely chop the mushrooms. Mince the garlic. In a medium sauté pan, heat 1 tablespoon of olive oil over medium heat and add the garlic and mushrooms. Season with salt, pepper, and a splash of dry white wine, and fry slowly until cooked.

Next, heat 1 tablespoon of olive oil and 1 tablespoon of butter in a large sauté pan. Coat the fillets of trout on one side in flour (placing the skin into the flour) and fry off quickly over high heat with the floured side down. Turn and again fry quickly (not to dry out the fish). Layer the fillets with the crispy, floured side upwards on a parchment-lined baking sheet and smear with the herb butter. Brown the top using high top heat until the herb butter foams up.

Add salt to the cooked mushrooms and sprinkle chopped parsley in last. Spoon mushrooms over the filets to serve. Carefully lift them out with a slotted spoon.

German Spätzle

Have fun and get the kids involved. Set the stage early in their development by letting them get their hands dirty. I have done this with both my children. It makes sensual learning applicable to daily life and memories along the way.

From Home Ec, otherwise known as family and consumer sciences, to experiencing it firsthand at a family-run pension near the Schwarzwald, or the Black Forest, spätzle can be bought or made at home. While the ingredients are not costly and rather essential, the technique makes these ununiform little shapes. Sauteed in butter with salt and pepper or dressed up in a cheese sauce with onions and bacon, spätzle is to Germany as pasta is a staple to Italy.

2 cups all-purpose flour

1 teaspoon sea salt

4 large eggs

½ cup whole milk

Bunch of parsley, chopped

Directions

In a mixing bowl, combine the flour, eggs, milk, and salt. Stir until the batter is well combined and develops bubbles. You can also use a mixer. The batter should neither be too thin nor too thick, or it won't be easy to make the spätzle. Let the batter sit for 5-10 minutes.

Bring a large pot of water to a boil over high heat, add about 1 tablespoon of salt, and reduce the temperature to a simmer. Press batter through a large, holed sieve or colander with a plastic spatula or wooden spoon into the simmering water. Perform this section in batches. After using about 1/3 of the batter, stop adding new spätzle and let them cook for about 2-3 minutes, or until they float to the top. Stir occasionally. Use a slotted spoon or a colander scoop to transfer the spätzle to a bowl to rest while making the remaining batches.

Serve the spätzle immediately or sauté them in butter to brown them a little. Finish with a handful of chopped parsley.

Linzer Cookies

A scaled-down version reminiscent of the decadent and decorative latticed Linzer Torte, these dainty cookies are perfect for an afternoon tea or special cup of joe. Not to mention they are Instagram-worthy.

In the dessert recipes that have made it into this book you will notice they are not overly sweet. That is on purpose and in line with how they are prepared in Europe. After living abroad, it is pretty apparent the differences culturally when it comes to baking. While there are incredible indulgences in France, Germany, Italy, and beyond, they are normally served in small portions versus their more mildly sweet treats that might be larger. In the US, our products are different and taste, which tends to see dessert lesser as an everyday occasion but consumed in celebration; some may reason make a case for more sugar.

In any circumstance, my recipes are inspired by my ventures living abroad and can give you a taste, living vicariously through every mouthful, of what it may feel like to have a crumpet in a bäckerei (bakery) in the heart of Berlin.

11/4 cups confectioners' sugar

1 cup almond flour

2 cups all-purpose flour

½ teaspoon salt

14 tablespoons cold unsalted butter, cubed

2 large egg yolks

1 teaspoon vanilla extract

½ teaspoon almond extract

Zest ½ lemon

½ cup raspberry jam

½ cup apricot jam

Directions

In the bowl of a food processor, process the sugar and almond flour until combined. Add the all-purpose flour, salt, and butter and pulse until the mixture resembles coarse crumbs, about twenty 1-second pulses. Add the egg yolks, vanilla, almond extract, and lemon zest and process until dough forms a crumbly, clumpy mass, 20 to 25 seconds. Transfer the dough to a clean work surface and knead it into a smooth ball. Divide the dough into two evenly portioned disks, wrap in plastic wrap, and refrigerate for at least 30 minutes.

Adjust the oven racks to the upper-middle and lower-middle positions and heat the oven to 375°F. Line two baking sheets with parchment paper.

Remove one disk of dough from the refrigerator and knead with your hands until just soft and malleable enough to roll. (The longer the dough is refrigerated, the more you will have to knead it; be careful not to overwork it – it should still feel cool.) Generously dust a clean work surface with flour and roll the dough to a ⅛-inch thick round. Using a 2.5-inch fluted edge, round cookie cutter, cut out circles. After creating the fluted edged cookies, use a 1-inch round, heart, or any-shaped cookie cutter to cut out the centers from half of the circles (these will be the top halves of the cookies).

Gently transfer the cookies to the prepared baking sheets, spacing about 1 inch apart.

Use the scraps, kneading them into a flat disc, roll, and repeat (if too warm, pop back in the fridge for a bit). Bake until the edges are lightly browned, about 8 minutes.

Let the cookies cool on the baking sheets for a few minutes, then transfer to a wire rack to cool completely.

Lightly sift confectioners' sugar over the cookie tops. Spread about 1 teaspoon jam on each base, leaving about a ¼-inch border, and sandwich both halves together. Store in an airtight container for up to 4 days.

Bavarian Cream

A light custard made with gelatin and whipped cream; this recipe can be consumed without abandon alone or stuffed into cakes, pastries, and donuts.

In the process of developing these recipes, I continued to make memories. Watching my son Henry taste goulash for the first time licking his lips with a satisfying grin or observing my husband reach for a second and then a third helping of Bavarian Cream were clear signs that I had perfected my creations.

As a chef or host of events or family gatherings, you will also find memory-making a multi-sensory experience. Feelings of joy and contentment are common when guests leave happy and gratified. That is one of the many reasons I love to entertain. I get to share a piece of myself with those gathered around the table.

Having a very human experience, I revel in positive feedback and praise.

1 teaspoon powder gelatin

2 large eggs separated

¼ cup sugar + 1 teaspoon

½ teaspoon vanilla

1 teaspoon orange liqueur

½ orange, zested

½ cup heavy whipping cream

Blueberry Coulis

2 cups frozen blueberries

¼ cup white wine

1 tablespoon sugar

½ orange zested

Directions

Add the gelatin along with 3 tablespoons of cold water to a pan. Let sit for 4 minutes.

While the gelatin is blooming, whisk the egg yolks with 1/4 cup sugar, vanilla, and orange liqueur until light in color and creamy. Whip the egg whites to stiff peaks and set them aside. In a separate bowl, whip the cream with the remaining 1 teaspoon sugar to stiff peaks. Set aside.

Heat the bloomed gelatin until just dissolved, 30 seconds to a minute. Slowly whisk the gelatin into the egg yolk mix. Whisk in the cream, followed by the egg whites.

Quickly pour the mix into individual glasses or a serving bowl. (Work fast as the gelatin will set relatively swiftly). Chill the Bavarian cream in the refrigerator for 1 hour or longer.

For the blueberry coulis, add the blueberries, sugar, wine, and orange zest to a saucepan and simmer until the sugar is dissolved. The blueberries will look soft and mushy (about 7-8 minutes).

Purée with a handheld immersion blender or regular blender and strain the liquid through a sieve. Let the coulis cool to room temperature, then cover, and store in the refrigerator until you're ready to use it.

Drizzle the coulis over the Bavarian cream right before serving. (The coulis will slowly "bleed" into the custard if it sits on it for long, so wait until service before spooning it on). Top with a dollop of whipped cream.

Mulled Wine | A Christmas Tradition

Sipping a warm spiced cup of red wine in front of the sundrenched Schönbrunn Palace in Vienna is one of my favorite Christmas memories of living in Europe.

On holiday visiting a mate, we had gone for a run on the palace grounds earlier in the day. We found ourselves returning to enjoy a typical yuletide pastime. Consumed by the season's merriment, with a crisp chill in the air and traditional Germanic music being played over the speaker, it wasn't hard to be seduced by the harmonious scene. Artisan vendors and irresistible delicacies, standing on the grand and opulent property once held by the Hapsburgs, I felt like I was living a fairytale. I had arrived. My dreams and aspirations culminated at this moment.

Those who have read my book Big Time Journey of a Small Town Girl, will understand this turning point.

Sometimes there will be moments in life that will stand out, where you will feel like everything has fallen into place.

This was one such realization; I was living the life I had experienced in my dreams.

2 (750 ml) bottles dry red wine

½ cup orange liquor (Grand Marnier or Triple Sec for example)

2 mandarins, sliced

10 whole cloves

3 cinnamon sticks

10 whole allspice

2-3 tablespoons raw honey

Directions
Combine 1 bottle of wine, orange liquor, mandarins, clove, cinnamon, allspice, and honey in a large saucepan. Stir to combine. Bring liquid to a simmer over medium-high heat, but do not boil. Reduce heat to low and cover. Let the wine simmer for 2 ½-3 hours. Pour the remaining bottle of wine in at the end and warm, keeping the alcohol content intact. Strain and serve with a cinnamon stick, orange slice, or twist of lemon.

Italy | Epicurean Way, All Roads Lead to Rome
A World of First Time Experiences

Studying culinary arts in the Cinque Terre, centuries-old villages that dot the Italian Riviera, I was immersed in Italy's decadence and splendor~ the sun, sand, and sea. Colorful houses with dark green shutters, vineyards clinging to the steep terraces, and little fishing boats nestled in the harbor. These five hamlets connected by a rail and a hiking path served as the backdrop to my culinary travels in 2005. After two years of studying hospitality and tourism at Kirkwood, I packed up my bags for a summer abroad. Starting in Tuscany and ending in Liguria, known for its coastal specialties, Chef Paolo Monti guided us through a prosciutto factory where the scent of salted pork wafted out the door and into the open air. Trying our hand at the antiquated practice of cheese making, we were directed to pick up a "spino," a traditional tool used to break up the larger mass of milk, rennet, and whey in the region Reggio-Emilia making Parmigiano-Reggiano.

Eating my fair share of gelato and tiramisu along the way, I had my first taste of Vin Santo dessert wine. The scent lingered on my lips as the taste of sun-drenched, raisin-like grapes danced on my tongue. To show restraint, I had none for *cantuccio*, the lesser-known word for biscotti that were so easily consumed standing at the neighborhood espresso bar, *al tavolo*, sheltering from the midday sun. "Let's get a coffee!" A *caffè* (or *caffè normale*), a simple espresso, is that pep-in-the-step pick me up appropriate any time of day. Get used to drinking it like the Italians or be cast as a foreigner. Forgoing the afternoon cappuccino is common practice amongst the locals, as milk and foam are believed to be a meal replacement and cause indigestion.

Porto Venere, situated on the Gulf of Poets, just south of the Cinque Terra, was where Chef Paolo Monti had his cooking school and welcomed us into his theatre for interactive demonstrations—first learning how to make risotto by ladling warm spoonfuls of broth over arborio rice. From the traditional asparagus listed in the pages that follow to more unique recipes that called for squid ink, truffle, beetroot juice, and goat cheese, the canvas of possibilities was left to the imagination. Stepping out of the airconditioned classroom looking out at the radiant spire of the Gothic-inspired church of St. Peter, we were encouraged to freely peruse the tiny shops and taste our way through artisan products.

Waking up each morning to small fishing boats lining the marina with the day's catch, I thought if this were heaven, I had arrived. Coursed lunches served with elegant wines from the countryside made living like a European a seductive experience. Every day finding enjoyment around the table without a rush to meet demands.

While Germany was the gateway into a parallel existence, Italy ushered in a new way of being. The power of firsts. I licked my plate and batted every dribble of sauce with crusty bread from the very beginning. The flavors are so pure and authentic, like capturing the essence of the farmer nurturing the vine—tomatoes bursting with ripeness and cheeses that tasted of tradition. Sitting for a cooking demonstration in a castle atop a hill, I can still remember the smoked mozzarella blanketed by thinly cut eggplant and baked with fresh marinara, an orgasmic epitome of the craft that is Italian gastronomy.

From seeing aromatic rosemary bushes growing like weeds to taking shots of homemade limoncello, my younger self was not afraid of the repercussion such extravagance would ensue, the string of firsts was easily woven. Squeezing our coach through traffic along winding streets to a lavish restaurant where the bathrooms were only outfitted with squat toilets to an agriturismo down a road lined with Italian cyprus, as you see in the movies. Wild boar so fragrant encrusted in robust herbs, this young American was in operation overload. At nineteen, one would legally abstain from sipping the nectar of the gods, but in Italy, one must do as the Italians do and accept the carafe of wine.

This wouldn't be my last trip to Italy. In 2013, after backpacking across Europe for five months, I found myself staying at a youth hostel in Rome. A friend I met through Couchsurfing in Bonn, Switzerland, visited the Italian capital on business. We met one balmy afternoon for an aperitif. A distinguishing Aperol Spritz in hand, we mused over the tantalizing delicacies displayed on the bar top served on individual plates waiting to be consumed. Out on the terrace, mingling with other locals and resident ex-pats alike, this bar was a neighborhood hangout with noteworthy fare. It was a jewel in the rough, as most of the best-kept secrets are.

Years later, my husband and I would also visit Rome. Provided with a cheat sheet from our Italian friend whom we met in Barcelona, we were guided on a culinary adventure. Having lived in Rome for twelve years, Andrea's recommendations were spot on, taking us to the outer suburbs for brunch, down dark pathways away from lively tourist traps to indiscrete doors, and places only reservations can be made by someone who knows someone. That is the way to travel- in-the-know, like the locals on one's quest for the extraordinary in the ordinary.

One of my bucket list items has been to travel from the top of the boot to the tip, from north to south, and onward to Sicily on a culinary quest to tantalize my tastebuds and make lasting memories. To go somewhere, I have not yet been. Many firsts still await.

Focaccia

A soft, chewy bread scented with rosemary, the taste of this sensational herb invigorates the mind as a drizzle of olive oil and sprinkling of flaky sea salt satisfy the palate.

Enjoyed sitting al fresco with ricotta salata, a hard, salted ricotta cheese eaten very young I was somewhere between Florence and Sienna staying at a fourth-century monastery converted to a makeshift youth hostel my friend was working at. I bought the cheese at the local supermarket. I thought the wedge would be more subtle like moist ricotta you might use in lasagna, but I was surprised. Sipping a delicately chilled pinot grigio, I remember the first bite and the saliva that formed as the salt hit my taste buds. The focaccia we bought to slurp up the sauce from our evening pasta was utterly necessary to bring balance to it all and be called bliss.

1 ⅓ cup warm water

(Approximately 110°F)

1 teaspoon honey

1 (0.25 oz) package active-dry yeast

2 cups all-purpose flour

1 ½ cup brown rice flour

¼ cup olive oil, plus additional

olive oil for drizzling

2-3 sprigs fresh thyme

2 sprigs fresh rosemary, half

reserved for garnish

2 teaspoons sea salt

1 teaspoon flaky sea salt for

garnish

Directions

Add honey to a large mixing bowl of warm water (about 110°F) and stir to combine. Sprinkle the yeast on top of the water. Give the yeast a gentle stir, and let it rest for 5-10 minutes until the yeast is foamy.

Gradually stir in the flours, olive oil, thyme, half the rosemary, and salt until a rough dough begins to form. Then turn the mixture onto a floured surface and knead by hand for five minutes until a smooth dough is formed, adding extra flour if the dough feels too sticky. Grease the mixing bowl with olive oil, then place the dough back in the bowl and cover it with a damp towel. Move the bowl to a warm spot in the kitchen and let the dough rise for 45-60 minutes, or until it has doubled in size. Turn the dough out onto a floured surface again and roll it out into a large circle or rectangle until the dough is about 1/2-inch thick. Cover the dough with a damp towel, and let it rise for another 20 minutes.

Preheat the oven to 400°F. Transfer the dough to a large parchment-covered baking sheet or round pizza pan. Use your fingers to poke deep dents, pressing all the way down to the baking sheet across the entire surface of the dough. Drizzle one to two tablespoons of olive oil evenly over the top of the dough, and sprinkle evenly with the remaining fresh rosemary needles and flaky sea salt.

Bake for 20 minutes, or until the dough is slightly golden and cooked through. Remove from the oven, and drizzle with more olive oil if desired. Slice, and serve warm.

Goat Cheese and Roasted Bell Pepper Crostini
This appetizer is for the goat cheese lovers. That includes me; I'm a glutton.

Whenever I see goat cheese on the menu, whether flambeed on a salad in France or as croquettes in Belgium, it grabs my attention and makes the decision a snap. It's that smooth, tangy flavor that, when paired with something sugary sings. While you might expect the traditional tomato basil bruschetta to grace these pages, this crostini turns heads. That right blend of sweet and savory with a drizzle of reduced balsamic gives it depth. My husband would say I am a balsamic vinegar junky; I would say there are worse things to be.

½ medium onion, sliced

1 teaspoon olive oil

1 teaspoon granulated sugar

1 jar roasted bell peppers, sliced

Sea salt

Freshly cracked black pepper (optional)

Reduced balsamic vinegar or balsamic glaze (optional)

1 small log (4 oz) natural goat cheese, room temperature

2 tablespoons Greek yogurt

Baguette, sliced and toasted

Directions
In a small bowl, cream together the goat cheese with the Greek yogurt. Set aside.

In a sauté pan over medium heat, warm the olive oil and add the onions and sugar. Sauté until translucent and lightly browned. Remove from heat and combine with the sliced bell pepper, a pinch of salt, and cracked black pepper.

Spoon a layer of goat cheese on the toasted slices of baguette and add a spoonful of the bell pepper mixture. Drizzle with reduced balsamic vinegar, store-bought or homemade.

Zucchini, Prosciutto, Arugula, and Apple Flatbread Pizza

**If you haven't experimented with different types of pizza, now is the time.
Give it a try and break away from your norm.**

Sometimes you don't want a chewy crust. That's where flatbread pizzas come in for a quick alternative. Lacking yeast, this pizza base takes no time to prepare in a food processor. Baked at 500 degrees, the crisp flatbread can be paired with the ingredients listed, or you can craft your flavor sensation.

While not traditionally popular in the States, Europeans will often sit down to their own 12-inch brick oven pizza and have no qualms about whether that was "healthy" or not. Across the Atlantic in Europe (excluding the U.K.), pizza served in restaurants is eaten with a fork and knife instead of your hands. It's not sliced and served hot, which is not conclusive to eating by hand. In general, the crust is different from "American" style pizza. It won't support the toppings the way heavily leavened dough does. Sometimes the pizza doesn't even have cheese on it. I tried a simple marinara pizza in Rome years back, and it was divine.

3 cups all-purpose flour

1 teaspoon table salt

1 cup warm water

3 tablespoons olive oil

Cornmeal for dusting

Desired toppings

Directions
Preheat the oven to 500ºF.

Add flour and salt to a food processor and pulse until well mixed. Add water and oil. Pulse until a dough ball forms (about 1 minute or so). Scrape down the sides as needed.

Transfer the dough ball to a lightly floured surface and knead the dough for 1 minute or until the surface of the dough is smooth. Divide dough into 2 equal balls. Use a rolling pin to roll each dough ball out into a long oval and to your desired thickness. Thinner is better in this case. Dust 2 baking sheets with cornmeal and place a flatbread crust on each. Poke the surface of the flatbread all over with a fork.

Bake the flatbreads for 7-9 minutes or until the flatbread edges turn golden brown and the flatbread is nearly cooked through. Brush with olive oil, top with desired toppings, and bake for another 5-10 minutes or so.

Toppings
Fresh mozzarella cheese ball, sliced
Fresh or store-bought pesto
Eggplant, thinly sliced, sprinkled with sea salt
Arugula greens
Prosciutto
Apple, sliced thin
Balsamic glaze

Pasta e ceci
Pasta and Chickpea Soup

As with most Italian soups, there is no one "right" recipe, but adaptations are made from family to family from generation to generation. This accessible soup uses on-hand ingredients to make a comforting dish in a flash. Hot foods, in general, do not have to be "scripted" 100 percent according to the recipe for them to come out sublime. Try a recipe once, then, like an artist, mix it up. Let your imagination guide you and your taste buds praise you.

1 medium onion, diced
1 clove garlic, minced
1 carrot, chopped
1 celery stalk, chopped
6 tablespoons olive oil, plus extra
for garnish
2 tablespoons tomato paste
1 teaspoon anchovy paste,
optional
1 sprig fresh rosemary
2 (14 oz) cans chickpeas, drained
½ cup white wine
4 cups vegetable stock
1 teaspoon sea salt
2 tablespoons fresh parmesan
2 flat dried lasagna sheets, broken
into small bits
Freshly cracked black pepper

Directions
Heat the olive oil to a medium temperature in a large, heavy pan. Add the onion, garlic, carrot, and celery and cook slowly until soft and fragrant. Add the tomato paste, anchovy paste, and rosemary. Stir to combine and continue cooking for 3-4 more minutes or until rosemary is fragrant. Add the drained chickpeas, white wine, vegetable stock, ½ teaspoon sea salt, and parmesan. Stir and bring to a gentle boil. Reduce the heat to a simmer for about 20 minutes.

Using an immersion blender or traditional blender, puree half the soup until creamy—return mixture to pan. Taste and adjust the salt according to your preference. Bring the soup back to a soft boil and add the broken pieces of pasta, stirring diligently until pasta is al dente. Add more stock if needed. Serve with a drizzle of olive oil and cracked black pepper.

Cioppino (Seafood Stew)

**Light and satisfying, this delectable stew can be made with the day's catch
or whatever favorite fresh fish you find at the market or store.**

Oddly enough, cioppino did not originate in Italy but was a concoction of Italian immigrants that settled in California and is most notable in the San Francisco Bay area. That is where I had my first dish. Flying solo, I landed in the NOMA area at a highly recommended restaurant bellied up at the bar top overlooking the chefs working in step in the open kitchen. Ever since I was a teenager, I have reveled in eating out on my own. Whether with a good book or conversing with a stranger, I love being in my own company. Egotistical, one might say, airing on the side of a confident foodie, I would have to lean.

2 tablespoons olive oil
1 fennel bulb, chopped
2 shallots, minced
2 garlic cloves, minced
3 sprigs fresh thyme
1 teaspoon dried oregano
¼ teaspoon red pepper flakes
Sea salt
Freshly ground black pepper
1 ½ cup dry white wine
1 (28-oz.) can crushed tomatoes
1 (15-oz.) can cherry tomatoes
1 (8-oz.) bottle clam juice
1 cup water
2 dried bay leaves
2 2"-thick strips orange zest
1 dozen littleneck clams, scrubbed
1 dozen mussels, scrubbed
1 lb. shrimp, peeled and deveined
1 lb. halibut, skin removed and
cut into 1" pieces
¼ cup freshly chopped parsley, for
serving
Baguette, for serving
Lemon wedges, for serving

Directions
Heat olive oil in a large pot over medium heat. Add fennel and shallots and cook until translucent, roughly 6 minutes. Add garlic, oregano, and red pepper flakes and season with salt and pepper. Cook 1 more minute.

Add white wine and let it boil reducing the liquid by half, 3 to 5 minutes. Pour in the tomatoes, clam juice, water, bay leaves, and orange zest. Stir to combine. Bring to a gentle simmer and cook uncovered for 20 minutes.

Remove bay leaves and orange zest. Add clams to simmering broth, cover, and cook for 5 minutes. Uncover, add mussels in an even layer, shrimp, and halibut. Do not stir. Cover the pot and cook for 5 more minutes, or until all clams and mussels are opened, and shrimp and fish are cooked. Remove and discard any unopened mussels and clams—season with salt and pepper to taste.

To serve, ladle soup into bowls and top with chopped parsley. Serve with a toasted baguette and lemon on the side.

Veggie & Brown Rice Frittata

Much like a quiche without the crust. A wonder of a dish that can capitalize on any leftovers in the fridge. While it's an egg-based dish, I serve this any time of the day, breakfast, lunch, or dinner.

Don't have brown rice, missing a vegetable? This recipe is one of the most forgiving. Utilize any leftovers you have in the refrigerator. Substitute the rice with faro, quinoa, barley, or the buttered pasta from last night. Missing zucchini? Grab the broccoli or spinach instead. This recipe is one of those dishes you can make at the end of the week to clear out the Tupperware in the refrigerator. Italians are big on not wasting the good stuff.

Even day-old bread is fair game. Plate it with some vine-ripened tomatoes and good quality olive oil and you have a masterpiece. Buon appetite!

1 tablespoon olive oil

2 ½ cup roasted vegetables, recipe below

¾ cup brown rice, prepared according to package recommendation

8 eggs

3 tablespoons milk or milk alternative

½ teaspoon sea salt

¼ teaspoon cracked black pepper

½ teaspoon oregano

½ teaspoon thyme

½ teaspoon smoked paprika

¼ teaspoon cumin

¼ cup Fontina cheese, crumbled, or any cheese you love

Directions

Preheat the oven to 400°F. In a medium-size non-stick sauté pan with a metal handle, sauté the roasted vegetables in olive oil. Using a small mixing bowl, crack the eggs, and whisk in the milk. Add the dry seasoning. Pour the egg mixture over the vegetables in the sauté pan until covered. Crumble the Fontina cheese over the top. Remove from the stovetop, and bake for 10-12 minutes until the top is golden brown, the cheese is melted, and the eggs have pulled away from the pan. Let cool for 5 minutes in the pan before sliding onto a cutting board or plate for service.

Roasted Vegetables

3 tablespoons olive oil
6 button mushrooms, sliced
1 zucchini, sliced
1 red pepper, julienned
1 yellow bell pepper, julienned
1 medium white onion, sliced
2 carrots, peeled and sliced
1 teaspoon sea salt
½ teaspoon black pepper

Directions

Preheat the oven to 425°F . In a large baking pan, combine all the vegetables. Toss in olive oil, salt, and pepper. Roast in the oven for 35-40 minutes, removing the baking dish every 12-15 minutes to stir. Pull the tender vegetables from the oven and transfer them to a medium-size non-stick sauté pan with a metal handle.

Parmigiana di Melanzane
Eggplant Parmesan

A genuine classic southern Italian dish that is adored around the world. So much so that it has spawned other variations of
"Parmesan"-style dishes that don't exist in Italy (or at least referred to as such), like chicken parmesan and veal parmesan.
This recipe asks for the eggplant to be baked rather than fried, a spin-off of the classic.
Altering the cooking method makes for a much healthier plate and leaves room for other tasty Italian temptations.

1 eggplant, sliced 1 cm thick rounds, salting both sides
½ cup flour
1 cup breadcrumbs
2 eggs
1 teaspoon dried oregano
1 teaspoon dried basil
½ teaspoon sea salt
1 tablespoon olive oil
2 cloves garlic, minced
1 carrot, sliced
1 stalk celery, chopped
1 small onion, chopped
¼ cup dry red wine
1 (15 oz) can fire-roasted tomatoes or diced tomatoes
1 ½ cup tomato sauce
2 tablespoons tomato paste
1 teaspoon dried oregano
½ teaspoon dried basil
½ teaspoon sea salt
¼ teaspoon ground black pepper
1 (15 oz) container part-skim Ricotta cheese
1 egg
¼ cup Parmesan cheese
¼ teaspoon sea salt

Directions

Slice and salt 1 cm thick eggplant rounds and let them rest on a plate for 30 minutes. While the eggplant is sweating, measure the flour, breadcrumbs, and egg into three separate bowls. Season the flour and breadcrumbs with ½ teaspoon of dried oregano, ½ teaspoon of dried basil, and ¼ teaspoon of salt. Whisk the eggs together and set them aside.

Preheat the oven to 400ºF and prepare a baking sheet with parchment paper.

Heat olive oil over medium heat in a medium-sized saucepan. Add the garlic and onions and sauté until translucent. Add the carrots and celery and cook for 5 minutes or until the carrots are tender. Pour in the wine, cooking until it is absorbed before adding the remaining ingredients, fire-roasted tomatoes, tomato sauce, tomato paste, oregano, basil, salt, and pepper. Bring to a simmer for 20 minutes before pureeing the sauce with a handheld immersion blender or use your traditional blender. Puree until a smooth, velvety sauce remains. Adjust the salt and pepper to taste.

After 30 minutes, pat the eggplant dry, removing any salt that remains. Drench the rounds first in flour, second in the egg wash, and lastly in the breadcrumb mixture before placing gently on the prepared baking sheet. Repeat this process for the entire eggplant. Place the eggplant in the oven and bake for 20 minutes.

While the eggplant bakes, prepare the ricotta, mixing the ricotta, egg, parmesan, and salt in a small bowl.

Remove the eggplant at the end of the first 20-minute baking period, and spoon a tablespoon of ricotta onto each eggplant round. Place the baking sheet back into the oven and cook for another 20 minutes or until the ricotta is set and slightly golden. Serve immediately, removing the baking sheet from the oven, plating the rounds over a ladle of sauce, and spooning additional sauce between each layer as you construct a napoleon, three or four layers high. Top with fresh basil and enjoy.

Fettuccini alla Puttanesca
Fettuccini with Shrimp, Olives, and Tomatoes

How can you pick just one pasta? You can't. So synonymous to Italy, pasta can take many forms, highlight endless combination of flavors, and be served as a primo, first course or appetizer, but is not likely to be the main, il secondo. While homemade pasta is celestial, not many of us have the time for this extra step and that's just fine. Buy a good quality fettuccini and make sure the pasta is al dente. Nestle the noodles in the sauce and let them lap up the goodness thickening the dish before service.

This recipe showcases that simplicity is an art. Extensive labor is not always necessary and that we can eat like kings every night of the week.

1 lb. fettuccini

3 tablespoons olive oil

¼ teaspoon crushed red pepper, optional

3 garlic cloves, minced

4 large Roma tomatoes, cut into ¼-inch dice

Sea salt

1 lb. medium shrimp, shelled and deveined, tails left on

⅓ cup kalamata olives, pitted and coarsely chopped

Freshly cracked black pepper, to taste

Pinch of dried oregano

½ cup fresh parsley, finely chopped

Directions

In a large pot of boiling salted water, cook the pasta until al dente. Reserve 1/2 cup of the pasta cooking water. Drain the pasta and return it to the pot.

Meanwhile, heat the olive oil in a medium skillet. Add the crushed red pepper (optional) and cook over low heat, stirring, for 30 seconds. Add the garlic and cook until fragrant, about 2 minutes. Stir in the tomatoes and cook over moderate heat for 3 minutes–season with salt. Add the shrimp and cook until they turn pink and curl, about 3 minutes. Stir in the olives and reserved pasta cooking water and cook until the sauce thickens slightly, about 2 minutes–season with salt and pepper. Toss the pasta with the sauce, pinch of oregano, and parsley to coat, transfer to a warmed bowl and serve.

Risotto with Asparagus

**In the world's rush, we could use a bit more of this –
time to enjoy, sit back, and be. If you haven't indulged in this custom, make it a first.**

After the coffee is served and maybe a digestif, you look at your watch and realize 4 or more hours have passed. Viva Italia!

On the weekend, family dinners, and especially on holidays, dinner can last into the night. Starting around 8 or 9 pm, and even later in the summer,

it is ubiquitous for Italians to enjoy multiple courses. There's no rush. The primo or first dish typically consists of risotto or pasta.

Whole servings of meat, like sausage, meatballs, or poultry, are customarily served as a secondo.

Approximately 4 cups of chicken or vegetable stock

2 tablespoons unsalted butter, divided

2 cloves garlic, minced

1 shallot, minced

½ medium onion, chopped fine

1 cup arborio rice

1 bay leaf

2 sprigs fresh thyme

¼ cup dry white wine

½ pound asparagus, washed, tips cut off, tough ends removed, and spears cut into thin disks

½ cup Parmesan, freshly grated cheese

Sea salt, to taste

Fresh ground black pepper, to taste

Directions

In a small saucepan, heat the stock over medium-high heat until it comes to a slow simmer.

In a separate 3- or 4-quart stock pot, melt 1 tablespoon of butter over medium heat. Add the garlic, shallot, and onion and cook until translucent. Add the arborio rice and cook for 2 minutes more, stirring gently to bring out the starch. Add the bay leaf, fresh thyme, and white wine. Slowly stir, allowing the rice to absorb the wine. Once the wine is almost entirely absorbed, add 1/2 cup of hot stock to the rice. Continue to stir until the liquid is almost completely absorbed, adding more stock in 1/2 cup increments. Stir frequently, preventing the rice from sticking to the bottom of the pan.

Continue cooking and stirring rice, adding a little bit of broth at a time until the rice is tender but still firm to the bite, about 20-25 minutes.

With the last addition of stock, add the asparagus. Stir and cook for a couple of minutes until the risotto has absorbed most of the stock, but is still loose, has a bit of liquid remaining, and the asparagus is still crisp. Turn the heat off. Gently fold in the Parmesan cheese and the remaining 1 tablespoon of butter. Add salt and pepper to taste. Serve immediately while rice is still al dente.

Osso Bucco

While it was only one night and one dish – the memory is still alive 15 years later.

The sauce, divine. The meat delicate and tender. An impression was made after my very first bite. A few years after studying in Italy, I celebrated my 22nd birthday on Mill Avenue a trendy student thoroughfare in Tempe, AZ near Arizona State University's central campus where I was a student. With reservations made at Cafe Boa, an eclectic, locally owned restaurant, serving up sumptuous experiences, I indulged my inner foodie. From wine to dessert, 22 would be a milestone I wouldn't forget.

4 thick veal shanks
Sea salt
Freshly ground black pepper
½ cup all-purpose flour
¼ cup olive oil
1 tablespoon unsalted butter
1 large yellow onion, diced fine
2 stalks celery, chopped fine
2 carrots, chopped fine
1 teaspoon dried oregano
1 teaspoon marjoram
1 ½ teaspoon sea salt
¾ cup dry white wine
2 tablespoons tomato paste
1 28-oz. can diced tomatoes
1 cup low-sodium chicken broth, plus extra as needed
1 large sprig thyme
1 bay leaf
1 tablespoon tapioca starch mixed with 2 teaspoons white wine
For the gremolata:
3 tablespoons finely chopped fresh flat-leaf parsley
2 large cloves garlic, minced
1 tablespoon finely grated lemon zest
1 ½- 2 teaspoons anchovy paste

Directions

Heat the oven to 350°F.

Tie the veal shanks around the center with kitchen twine, making a cross before knotting, and season them with salt and pepper. Put the flour in a dish. Dredge the shanks very lightly in flour and thoroughly pat off the excess.

Prepare a large roasting pan or baking dish to hold the shanks in a single layer. Heat 3 tablespoons of the oil over medium-high heat in a large heavy skillet. Put two veal shanks in the pan and sear until browned on both sides (2 to 3 minutes per side). Transfer the shanks to the roasting pan and repeat the other two shanks.

Carefully pour off the fat in the pan and wipe it out with paper towels. Some of the browned bits will remain, and that's fine. Return the pan to the stovetop over medium to medium-low heat and melt the butter with the remaining tablespoon of olive oil. Add the onion, celery, carrot, oregano, marjoram, and 1 teaspoon of sea salt. Cook the vegetables, occasionally stirring, until soft and lightly browned, 15 to 20 minutes. Increase the heat to medium-high, add the wine, stir, and cook, until the wine is reduced to about 1/4 cup, or approximately 3 minutes.

Stir in the tomato paste. Add the can of tomatoes, broth, thyme, bay leaf, 1/2 teaspoon sea salt, and a few cracks of black pepper. Bring the mixture to a boil. Turn off the heat and pour over the shanks. Cover tightly with heavy-duty aluminum foil or oven-safe cover.

Braise the veal in the oven until fork-tender, 1-1/2 to 2 hours, checking the liquid occasionally. If it has cooked down, add enough broth to keep the level about halfway up the shanks. To check for doneness, pierce a shank with a fork. The meat should pull apart easily. Taste a morsel–it should feel soft and tender. Do not overcook, or the veal will fall apart.

Before finishing the sauce and serving, combine the parsley, garlic, lemon zest, and anchovies. Add two tablespoons of the gremolata to the sauce. Remove the strings from the shanks. Serve the osso bucco topped with the sauce and a small sprinkling of the remaining gremolata.

Tiramisu

If you ever visit Phoenix, stop by Va Bene Restaurant. On the outer fringes of suburbia, this Italian wine bar and eatery has some of the best Italian food outside Italy I have ever tasted. Their homemade gnocchi taste like little pillows of heaven tossed in a vodka sauce that is the type of sauce you ask for the recipe in hopes of recreating a masterpiece at home. Bragging aside, my friends own this little prize, and I helped shake drinks and serve tables for a stint. Now you can imagine if their hot foods are tempting, their desserts are even better. Paired with a tawny port, the tiramisu is made in-house, and the union satiates every tastebud with delight.

4 large egg yolks
½ cup sugar, divided
¾ cup heavy whipping cream
1 cup mascarpone
1 ½ cup espresso
1 mandarin, juiced
2 tablespoons unsweetened cocoa powder
Approximately 24 ladyfingers

Directions

In a large bowl, whip together egg yolks and ¼ cup sugar until pale in color and about triple in size. In a separate bowl using an electric hand mixer, beat the heavy whipping cream and remaining ¼ cup sugar until soft peaks form. Add the mascarpone and continue to whip until it creates a smooth, spreadable mixture. Gently fold the mascarpone mixture into the beaten egg yolks until combined and set aside.

Pour espresso and mandarin juice into a shallow bowl.

Using a small sifter, dust the bottom of your 8 x 8" baking dish (9 x 7" baking dish or 9" round dish) with 1 tablespoon cocoa powder.

For assembly, quickly dip each lady's finger into the espresso mixture and place them dip-side up into the serving dish.

Finish the first layer and spread half of the mascarpone mixture over the ladyfingers. Repeat dipping the ladyfingers and arrange a second layer. Top with the rest of the mascarpone mixture. Cover with plastic wrap and let rest in the refrigerator at least 4 hours before serving. Ideally, let it set and chill for 24 hours before slicing.

Orange, Almond & Cranberry Biscotti
Delectable on their own, you won't be able to stop at just one.

Hosting a holiday cookie lalapalooza in our Barcelona flat, members of the International Women's Club of Barcelona trickled in to stir, crack, whisk, and bake. Being a passion of mine, baking, that is, it was a joyous morning concocting traditional favorites with a slightly healthy twist. While there was another women's networking group in Barcelona, IWCB made me feel like I belonged. Women, primarily British, American, and Catalan pensioners, were warmhearted and full of vitality having chosen to retire in one of Europe's prized holiday destinations. Long a part of Barcelona's dynamic fabric, these women were my lifeblood while I wrote my first book and transitioned from one professional endeavor to the next.

That day, four cookies, molasses ginger snaps, sandies, cut-out cookies, and these twice-baked, crunchy favorites were on the menu. Try them with a shot of espresso or a Spanish cortado. Better yet, take a break in the afternoon and do as the Italians and Spaniards do, rest with a glass of wine in hand and dip the cookie in. Savor the burst of life that awakens the senses and do it again.

4 tablespoons cold unsalted butter, cubed

⅓ cup coconut sugar

¼ cup white sugar

2 eggs

1 mandarin, zested, and juice half

½ teaspoon vanilla extract

½ teaspoon almond extract

1 teaspoon baking powder

½ teaspoon sea salt

1 cup all-purpose flour

1 cup whole wheat flour

½ cup almond slivers

½ cup dried cranberries

Directions

Preheat the oven to 350° F. Line a baking sheet with parchment paper. Using an electric mixer, beat the butter and sugar together until creamy. Add the eggs, zest, mandarin juice, vanilla, and almond extract; mix until well combined.

Stir together the all-purpose flour, whole wheat flour, baking powder, and salt in a medium bowl. Add the flour mixture to the mixing bowl and mix on low speed until combined, scraping down the sides of the bowl.

Divide the dough in two. Shape each half into a ball and use your hands to shape each ball into an 8-inch log about 2-inches wide. The logs will be about 3/4-inch thick. Gently even out the ends into a flush rectangle with slightly rounded edges.

Bake for 20-25 minutes until lightly golden and the center of the logs is almost firm. Let the logs cool on the baking sheet for 30 minutes.

Using a sharp knife, cut the logs into biscotti shapes on the diagonal. Press straight down with the blade rather than using a serrated edge.

Place the biscotti, cut side up, on the baking sheet. Bake for 15-20 more minutes until dry. The centers of the cookies will be slightly soft and will be crisp as they cool. Store biscotti in an airtight container at room temperature for 1-2 weeks or in the freezer for three months.

Strawberry Balsamic Crumble with Vanilla Ice Cream or Greek Yogurt sweetened with Honey and Cardamom

On the last night of our travel studies in Italy in Porto Venere, Chef Paolo Monti provided one final cooking demonstration which would become the crème de la creme. A big bowl of sliced strawberries adorned the table as Chef began to drizzle an aged balsamic from Modena onto the fruit. With a few cranks of the pepper mill, the strawberries no longer resembled your run-of-the-mill store-bought pint but were supercharged. While vinegar and pepper sound off-putting and one might be cautious to try, the combination intensifies the flavor of the berry. Suppose you're serving picky or non-adventurous eaters.

In that case, you might want to keep this secret to yourself until after they've raved about the taste.

Quickly a summer favorite of mine, we'll fast forward time. Preparing an online cooking class for a corporate client that would be both healthy and seasonal, I took inspiration from that sumptuous night. A unique crumble, a blend of cultures, epitomizes summer and provides that sweet but not too sweet finish that guests will praise.

2½ cups quartered strawberries

1 teaspoon balsamic vinegar

¼ teaspoon cardamom

⅓ cup whole rolled old fashioned oats

⅓ cup chopped pecans

¼ cup almond flour*

2 tablespoons maple syrup

½ teaspoon cinnamon

⅛ teaspoon sea salt

1 tablespoon coconut oil

Vanilla ice cream or natural yogurt from soy, almonds, or unsweetened Greek yogurt for serving (sweeten the yogurt slightly with a good quality honey)

Directions

Preheat the oven to 375°F.

In the bowl of a food processor, pulse the oats, pecans, flour, cinnamon, and salt until just combined. Add the maple syrup and coconut oil and pulse again. The mixture should be crumbly.

Combine the strawberries with balsamic vinegar and cardamom in a medium bowl. Divide the strawberries between four small ramekins for baking or two mini skillets. Top with the crumble.

Bake 15 minutes or until the fruit is bubbly and the topping is lightly browned. Remove from the oven and let cool for 10 minutes. Serve with vanilla ice cream or a spoonful of Greek yogurt sweetened with honey.

Alternatively, this can be served unbaked. Sprinkle the crumble over the fresh strawberries and top with a dollop of yogurt if desired.

England & Ireland | "God Save The Cream"
Memories are Made in the Details

A month in Italy led to a summer in England in 2004. Continuing my culinary travel studies, I worked for Drayton Court, a pub operated by Fuller, Smith, and Turner on London's West End. A Michelin starred chef was found burrowed in the kitchen downstairs and levied up the most delectable fare on a lift, aka elevator, where staff would carry it to hungry patrons.

Arriving a little after midnight in an iconic black cab from Saint Pancreas train station, I was fortunate to find employees still enjoying the fruits of their labor, sipping beverages guests had tipped them. It is common practice in Britain to tip a bartender a libation rather than a quid (pound sterling) for service. At nineteen years old, above the legal age to drink in the U.K., I found this a great repose from a bustling night. And so, travel-weary from a day's voyage by train from Italy, I had arrived for my summer internship.

A first for the community college where I studied culinary arts, it was on the dean's approval that I would embark on an international internship, and the head of the hospitality program was charged with providing me with coursework. From learning how to change beer taps and being tasked with cleaning the pipes every fortnight, I discovered what it took to be a British bartender. Where a *blasé* attitude was not so far off the mark, and quite the opposite to the genial temperament one expects from a server in the U.S. Tips were not expected, but drinks were enjoyed. At nineteen years old, my first experience in London was full of mixed emotions. The cultural component was enveloping. From behind the bar, I had to translate thick English accents with no resemblance to what I thought was being conveyed into drinks for thirsty guests. Across from the pub was an Indian takeaway where in a quick fix after a shift, I could take a plate of curry up to my room in a sequestered hotel that had once seen its glory, outfitted to be staff quarters. Not one for cleanliness, there was very little management of the lodging, and I had a stint stricken by bedbugs. That is a memory I would like to forget and one that would ultimately cut my internship short. But why dwell upon discomfort when there are so many highlights to the memory reel?

From London's Chinatown to Camden's quirky shops and oh, so yummy food stalls, many culinary experiences can be classified as "out-of-the-ordinary." If it is your first time in London, everything is a bit novel. As with most notable European cities, you must get off the beaten path and away from the hordes of tourists to find the real British experience. That is not to say that a lavish meal at the Savoy doesn't leave an incredible impression. It indeed does, especially after a visit to the theatre.

On a weekend to Galway and up the coast to Sligo, we took the back roads, winding through small towns along the Irish coast. I tasted my first caramel shortbread at a little bakery across from the bed and breakfast where we stayed. Greeted by Irish hospitality, there was no way one could go hungry.

From tasting whiskey at Bushmills Distillery, a stop on a bus tour of Giant's Causeway, to sitting at the Smithwick's Brewery only months before it was sold to Guinness and production in Kilkenny was moved to Dublin, memories come flooding back as I write. A story, a scent, the view—fostering awareness of the present moment can enhance the experience and make it even more possible to retrieve the memory.

Enjoying a pint at the Gravity Bar, taking in 360° views of Dublin at the Guinness Storehouse, I realized my return flight to the United States was taking off from Charles de Gaulle Airport outside Paris. Against what some might call "better judgment," I would backpack across Europe on my own rendition of *Eat, Pray, Love*. While immersed in the sights, history, and distinct flavors of one of the world's most famous beers, I stood in awe and a bit of fear at the journey ahead. By deciding to forgo returning to the United States that day, having traveled to Ireland instead of France, I adopted a new trajectory into the future. This layer of realization paired with such a unique environment was unforgettable, striking not only a physical cord of memory but that of emotion as well.

One of the different types of memories, *emotional memories*, denote events that elicit an expressive response during the occasion or incident. Brown and Kulik coined the phrase "flashbulb memory," in which they argued that when a highly surprising or unusual event occurs or a significant life event, like having a baby, a unique memory mechanism is sparked, causing the moment to be recorded with picture-perfect accuracy. [i]

Allow yourself to feel. Be taken by the moment. Travel with abandon. Arms wide open. Consume ready to receive. Let yourself feel in order to remember.

Irish Leek and Potato Soup

Rain, rain go away, come again another day, but wait, not before soup. Countries not renowned for their idyllic weather, you never want to leave the house without an umbrella. With a temperate climate, that does boast four seasons and never teeters in the extremes, one can always find an excuse to pour a cup of tea and consume what many would consider quintessential comfort food. Whether it is rainy and grey outside or a sliver of sunshine peaks through the clouds and a picnic is ready to be had, you will find this recipe is ready to be taken on-the-go or enjoyed at home.

2 tablespoons unsalted butter

½ small onion, chopped

3 cloves garlic, chopped

2 leeks, chopped (about 3 cups)

3 cups Yukon yellow potatoes

2 bay leaves

½ teaspoon ground marjoram

1 teaspoon dried thyme

1 teaspoon sea salt

¼ teaspoon ground black pepper

6 cups chicken stock

½ cup cream

Directions

In a large pot, begin to sauté the onions and butter in melted butter for 1-2 minutes. Add the leeks. Continue to cook for 8-10 minutes over medium heat. Add the potatoes and seasoning, bay leaves, marjoram, thyme, salt, and pepper.

Cook for a minute or two to release starch from the potatoes. Add the stock and bring to a rolling simmer for 20 minutes. Remove from heat and puree until smooth. Add the cream and serve. Adjust the seasoning according to taste.

Cornish Pasties

From the classic stuffing to more modern takes on this convenient, on-the-go hand pie, this dish can be a whole meal in one. Made to be eaten warm or cold, you can take them to the office, a picnic or heat it on a plate and serve it with Britain's iconic baked beans and pint. I love grabbing these at farmer's markets or from a food stall in the eclectic Brixton Market, a multicultural area that boasts down-to-earth Caribbean vibes. A melting pot, much like the rest of London, this cool hangout known by locals and tourists alike is fizzing with quirks, character, and some of the best, authentic food finds. Whenever I am in London Town, I make it a priority to get my fix, and if I am with friends, we make a night of it listening to music, tarrying in and out of colorful restaurants and cafés along narrow walkways in this exciting hub.

For the pastry

2 cups all-purpose flour

½ cup cold unsalted butter, cubed

¾ teaspoon sea salt

½ cup cold water

Filling

1 pound flank steak, cubed small

1 cup rutabaga, peeled and cubed small

1 cup yellow potatoes, peeled and cubed small

½ medium onion, minced

1 teaspoon sea salt

1 teaspoon dried thyme

Hefty crank of cracked black pepper to taste

1 egg

Directions

In a large pot, use a pastry cutter to cut the cold cubes of butter into the flour and salt until small pea-like shapes form. Alternatively, you can use a food processor, putting the flour, salt, and butter into the processor and pulsing until the same pea-sized shapes are formed. Using your hands, fork, or continuing with the food processor, slowly add the water until a dough ball is formed. Not all the water may be needed. Wrap the dough in plastic wrap and chill in the refrigerator for at least 15 minutes.

Preheat the oven to 425ºF. Prepare a large baking sheet with parchment paper.

While the dough chills, prepare the filling. Add the cubed rutabaga, potato, flank steak, onion, and seasoning into a large mixing bowl. Stir until evenly combined.

When the dough has finished chilling, remove it to a floured surface–divide the dough into eight equal balls. Roll each piece into rounds the size of a tea plate–approximately 6 to 7 inches in diameter. Divide the meat mixture evenly among each pastry round and place it on one side. Brush the edges with the beaten egg.

Fold the circle in half over the filling, so the two edges meet. Crimp the edges together to create a tight seal. This can be done with your fingers or a fork. Brush each pasty with the remaining beaten egg. Place the pasties on the baking sheet and bake for 20 minutes. Lower the oven temperature to 350ºF and bake another 20 minutes until golden brown. Serve hot or cooled.

Pecan Meatless Meatloaf
Kilkenny

Laboring over maps, I have tried to find the café in Kilkenny I visited twice for this with no resolve, but in trying to recreate the taste and texture of this dish, I think I got close. The addition of cinnamon and nutmeg sounds weird but provides the most unique flavor that makes this meatless meatloaf so interesting and captivating. When you eat plant-based or vegan, you need to lean on herbs and spices to doctor things up and make them exciting.

Tasty temptations are memorable, and this recipe earns the trophy.

½ cup pecan pieces
½ cup cashews
1 tablespoon salted pumpkin seeds
1 tablespoon olive oil
8-ounce package button or cremini mushrooms
½ large white onion
2 cloves garlic
2 medium roasted sweet potatoes, approximately 1 cup
⅔ cup unseasoned breadcrumbs
1 egg
1 tablespoon soy sauce
½ teaspoon thyme
½ teaspoon oregano
½ teaspoon marjoram
½ teaspoon rosemary
1 teaspoon sage
1 teaspoon paprika
¼ teaspoon cinnamon
¼ teaspoon nutmeg
Sea salt & cracked black pepper to taste

Sauce
¼ cup tomato paste
1 ½ tablespoon apple cider vinegar
1 tablespoon soy sauce
1 tablespoon maple syrup
¼ teaspoon garlic powder
⅛ teaspoon paprika
Sea salt & cracked black pepper to taste

Directions

Prep in advance- 2 medium sweet potatoes. Wash and place them in a small baking dish. Cover them with aluminum foil and bake in an oven at 425ºF for 50 minutes to an hour. The sweet potatoes will be soft throughout. Remove the peels and mash with a fork.

When ready to make the loaf, toast the raw pecans and cashews in the oven at 325ºF for 10 minutes. After removing the nuts, preheat the oven to 350ºF for the loaf.

Add the pecans, cashews, and pumpkin seeds to a food processor and pulse to a coarse meal with a few larger pieces throughout. Pour the mix into a large mixing bowl.

Add your mushrooms, onion, and garlic in the same food processor. Pulse until minced. Heat a skillet over medium heat.

Drizzle in the olive oil, spoon in the mushroom mixture, and cook until the moisture from the mushrooms has cooked off and the mix starts to brown around the edges. Combine this in with the nuts in the large mixing bowl. Grab your prepared sweet potatoes and add this to the bowl as well—season with all the spices, salt, and cracked black pepper. Add the soy sauce, egg, and breadcrumbs and mix well.

Taste and adjust salt, herbs, and flavor. The flavor will get more intense while baking. If the mixture is too wet, add an additional spoon or two of breadcrumbs. You want it to be slightly sticky. If it's too dry or crumbly, add a splash of vegetable broth.

Transfer the meatloaf mixture to a parchment-lined loaf pan. Lightly press to shape and even it out. Do not press it down too firmly. Bake for 25 minutes. Meanwhile, mix all of the ingredients for the glaze in a small bowl. Taste and adjust if needed. Take the loaf out of the oven after time has elapsed, add the sauce, and bake again for 35 minutes. Let cool for 15 minutes before removing it from the pan. Cool completely before slicing.

Cottage Pie (Ground Beef) Shepard's Pie (Ground Lamb)

My Grandma Lois was notorious for making her rendition of Shepard's Pie. With ground beef, frozen sweet corn, and a thick tomato sauce, the potatoes would be blanketed by thick slices of Velveeta cheese. Not so traditional, but it drew the family together. After working in London and traveling extensively around Ireland, when I make this dish served with a pint of ale, I am transported back to a dimly lit, wood-heavy public house so full of good cheer and merriment. A staple in the British and Irish way of life is the congenial feeling of having a place. Families convene on Sunday for brunch or wind down from a hard day midweek in this neighborhood bar. Even if you're sipping a simple tonic, the public house is an institution, and cottage pie is a portal into remembering.

1 ½ tablespoon olive oil
2 garlic cloves, minced
1 onion, finely chopped
1 carrot, finely chopped
1 stalk celery, finely chopped
2 lb. ground beef
¼ cup all-purpose flour
6 ounce can tomato paste
2 cups beef stock
½ cup dry red wine
1 beef bouillon cube
2 tablespoons Worcestershire sauce, low sodium
1 teaspoon dried thyme
1 teaspoon marjoram
2 bay leaves
1 teaspoon salt
¼ teaspoon ground black pepper
½ cup frozen sweet peas
¼ cup frozen sweet corn
Topping
5 large Russet potatoes, peeled and cut into 1" cubes
¼ cup Greek yogurt
¼ cup milk
1 tablespoon unsalted butter
Salt & pepper to taste
2 tablespoons butter
2 tablespoons English Cheddar cheese, grated

Directions

Heat oil in a large skillet over medium-high heat. Add onion and garlic, and cook for a minute before adding the carrots and celery. Cook until the vegetables are tender.

Turn the heat up to high and add the beef. Cook until browned.

Stir in the flour until combined. Add the tomato paste, broth, red wine, bouillon cube, Worcestershire sauce, thyme, marjoram, bay leaves, salt, and pepper.

Bring the mixture to a simmer, turning down the heat to medium-high. Cook for 30 minutes, occasionally stirring, until it reduces to a gravy consistency. Taste, adding more salt if desired.

Transfer the mixture to a 1.5 liter/quart baking dish. Cover, cool if you have time (even overnight). Cooling the filling will make spreading the mashed potatoes over the gravy mixture easier.

Assembly

Preheat the oven to 350°F.

Cook potatoes in boiling water for 15 minutes or until soft and fork-tender. Drain, then return to a pot on the turned-off stovetop. Add butter and mash until melted, then add milk and salt. Mash until smooth.

Spread or pipe the mashed potatoes onto the pie, and use a fork to rough up the surface, enhancing the browning. Sprinkle with cheddar cheese, and drizzle with butter.

Bake for 25 - 30 minutes or until golden on top and bubbling on the edges. Stick a knife into the middle to ensure it is piping hot.

Let the baking dish stand for 5 minutes before serving, garnished with fresh thyme leaves or chopped parsley if preferred.

Slow Cooked Corn Beef and Cabbage

My father always loved corned beef hash, essentially sauteed onions, cubed potatoes, and corned beef. Simple and delicious, yet I just didn't get it until I found myself in a pub on yet another rainy day somewhere between Galway and Sligo on the West Coast of Ireland. While hash wasn't on the menu, normally a breakfast item, the all popular corned beef and cabbage was. This is when the light bulb went on. Funny, when we are kids, we often have picky tendencies. Whether influenced by our classmates at school, our unsophisticated tastebuds or lack of wanting to eat "green things," we often miss out on some pretty extraordinary food. I am glad life gave me another encounter with this dish, because quite frankly, I may have never made it on my own. Think about what you disliked as a child and come back to it. Take one bite as I tell my children and then judge; you may be pleasantly surprised things have changed.

2 pounds corned beef (with seasoning packet that is included)
1 tablespoon brown sugar
2 bay leaves
2 cloves garlic, peeled and halved
Beef stock
3 carrots
3 potatoes
1 medium head of cabbage
2 tablespoons butter
1 tablespoon flour
1 tablespoon honey
¼ cup horseradish
1 tablespoon Dijon mustard

Directions

Place the brisket, contents of the accompanying seasoning packet, brown sugar, bay leaves, and garlic in a large stockpot, cover the meat with water, and bring it to a boil. Reduce heat and bring the liquid to a simmer for 2 hours, covered.

Add the potatoes and carrots and return the cooking liquid to a boil again. Reduce heat; simmer covered until beef and vegetables are tender, 30-40 minutes. (If the pot is full, remove the potatoes and carrots before adding the cabbage; reheat everything before service.)

Add cabbage to the pot; return to a boil. Reduce heat; simmer covered until cabbage is tender, about 5 minutes. Remove the vegetables and corned beef, covering it with foil to keep it warm.

For the horseradish sauce, strain and reserve 1-1/2 cups of the cooking liquid; skim fat from the reserved juices. Discard the remaining liquid. In a small saucepan, melt the butter over medium heat, and whisk in the flour until smooth. Gradually incorporate 1 cup of reserved juices while continuing to whisk. Stir in the honey, mustard, and horseradish; bring the sauce to a boil, constantly stirring until thickened. Thin the sauce with additional cooking liquid and season to taste with extra honey, vinegar, or horseradish.

Cut the beef across the grain into slices. Serve with the cooked vegetables and a ramekin of sauce.

Teatime Sandwiches

That moment when every taste bud is tickled, and you feel as though you are walking on clouds. The simple things in life are often the most profound.

Having been invited to London for an International Spa Awards Ceremony, a luxurious afternoon was carved out to indulge in the truly British pastime of afternoon tea at the Sofitel St. James. A classic three-tiered tray or "curate" on which three savory courses were served was followed by delectable petit fours. To top the lavish affair, champagne was served with the quintessential cup of Earl Grey tea, making it a 'Royal Tea' denoting the extravagance of the occasion. Highbacked chairs, elegant décor, the height of sophistication, you could imagine women in their petticoats and the coherently British bowler hats from the Victorian era sitting amongst high society sipping tea. Whether replicating this ceremonious affair at home or partaking in a tea house that specializes in such refinements, do yourself the compliment, partake.

Egg Salad Sandwich

5 hard-boiled eggs
¼ cup mayonnaise
1 stalk celery, chopped fine
1 green onion, sliced
1 teaspoon fresh dill, chopped fine
1 teaspoon fresh parsley, chopped fine
2 teaspoon Dijon mustard
⅛ teaspoon smoked paprika
⅛ teaspoon sea salt
Cracked black pepper

Smoked Salmon, Cucumber, and Cream Cheese Sandwich

2 ounces of cream cheese, room temperature
1 ½ tablespoons Greek yogurt
1 clove garlic confit (see recipe on page 86)
1 teaspoon fresh dill, chopped fine
¼ teaspoon lemon zest
Sea salt and pepper to taste

For the sandwich:
Sandwich bread, thinly sliced raisin bread was used here
Smoked salmon, good quality, thinly sliced
English cucumber, sliced thinly lengthwise the width of the sandwich

Directions for the Egg Salad Sandwich

Gently place the eggs in a medium pot and cover entirely with water. Bring the water to a boil, turn off the heat and cover the eggs for 12 minutes. Drain the hot water and run cold water over the eggs, letting them cool entirely before cracking and removing the shell.

When the eggs are cooled, remove the shell, run under water, and pat dry. Chop the eggs into small pieces. Add the egg and the list of remaining ingredients into a mixing bowl and stir to combine. Taste and adjust salt and pepper according to your preference.

Spoon a good amount of egg salad on a thin slice of bread (It's your choice here. The classic is white bread, but I usually go for the healthier seedy variety.) Add the second slice of bread on top and cut it evenly down the middle. Cut it again if more petite sandwiches are desired. The crust may also be removed.

Directions for the Smoked Salmon, Cucumber, and Cream Cheese Sandwich

In a small mixing bowl, combine the cream cheese, Greek yogurt, and clove of garlic confit. Blend until smooth. Add the dill, lemon zest, salt, and pepper. Taste and adjust seasoning. Spread a generous spoon of cream cheese dill spread over both pieces of the bread evenly. Layer the cucumber and sliced salmon on top one slice and cover it with the other. Slice lengthwise.

Sticky Toffee Pudding

The fragrant aroma, the rich flavor, the caramel color, every morsel is sweet and divine.

Toffee, in general, gets me weak in the knees. It gives me all the feels. It takes me back to eloquent tea gardens and centuries-old pubs. One bite, eyes closed, my imagination can render any past experience as vivid as the day it was lived. Enraptured in memory, time stands still, and life feels fuller.

You know the feeling of contentment after a Thanksgiving feast. That's it—pure bliss.

15-20 Medjool dates, chopped
¾ cup boiling water
1 teaspoon baking soda
5 tablespoons unsalted butter
2 tablespoons molasses
1/3 cup dark brown sugar, packed
2 eggs, room temperature
1 teaspoon vanilla extract
¼ teaspoon nutmeg
1 cup whole wheat flour
1 teaspoon baking powder
¼ teaspoon sea salt

Toffee Sauce
½ cup unsalted butter
¾ cup heavy whipping cream
¾ cup dark brown sugar, packed
2 tablespoons molasses
Pinch sea salt
½ teaspoon vanilla
Squeeze ½ mandarin juice

Garnish
1 cup heavy whipping cream
1/8 teaspoon ground cardamon
1 mandarin zest

Directions

Cake
Preheat the oven to 350°F. Chop the dates, approximately 1 cup, and place them in a cereal bowl. Cover with boiling water and sprinkle the baking soda over the top. Let set for 20 minutes.

Creaming the butter, brown sugar, and molasses in a mixing bowl until creamy. Add the eggs one at a time, incorporating them into the butter well between each one. Stir in the vanilla.

Combine the flour, nutmeg, baking powder, and sea salt in a separate bowl. Slowly add the flour mixture to the butter mixture until combined. After the dates have soaked for 20 minutes, puree them using an immersion blender or small food processor. Transfer the puree of dates into the cake batter and stir to combine.

Butter 9-12 count muffin tin. Using an ice cream scoop, evenly spoon the batter into the individual cups, approximately 3/4 way full. Bake 20-25 minutes, being careful not to overbake. Remove from the oven and flip onto a wire rack to cool.

Toffee Sauce
In a medium saucepan over medium heat, melt the butter. Add the cream, brown sugar, molasses, and salt. Bring the mixture to a simmer, whisking occasionally for 7-8 minutes. Whisk in the vanilla and mandarin juice and set aside. The sauce will thicken as it cools.

Whipped Cream Garnish
In a cold metal mixing bowl, whisk the whipping cream until thick. Add the cardamon and mandarin zest and set aside for plating.

Assembly
While the cakes are still warm, remove them from the muffin tin and, using a serrated knife, trim off the domed muffin top. Place cut side down on the cooling rack resting atop a baking sheet. Slowly pour the toffee sauce over each cake, reserving the remaining sauce for plating.

Serve the cakes warm, drizzled with extra toffee sauce and a large dollop of whipped cream.

Raisin Scones

After hiking Croagh Patrick, one of Ireland's most stunning low-lying mountains with a unique conical shape towering above Clew Bay, we stopped at an old inn on the outskirts of Murrisk. Being the middle of the afternoon after an earlier rain, we were the only guests of the proprietors. A self-professed connoisseur of scones, we ordered two. Served warm with homemade strawberry jam and clotted cream, a third was compulsory to recoup the calories we burned on our 4-hour pilgrimage to the small church on the summit. Maybe it was the exhilaration from the 764-meter assent over 4.31 miles or the fact these scones were some of the best I have ever tasted that warranted the splurge.

1 cup all-purpose flour
¼ cup sugar
1 tablespoon baking powder
¼ teaspoon sea salt
½ cup unsalted butter, cubed
⅓ cup Greek yogurt
¼ cup milk
1 teaspoon vanilla
1 cup raisins
1 egg yolk, beaten for egg wash

Directions

Preheat the oven to 400ºF.

Combine the flour, sugar, baking powder, and salt in a food processor. Add the cubed butter and pulse until pea-sized crumbs form. Add the egg, vanilla, and Greek yogurt until combined. Add the milk slowly. Remove the mixture from the processor and fold in the raisin on a lightly floured surface.

Roll out the dough to 3/4-inch thickness. Using a round cookie cutter, cut out the scones. Continue until almost all the dough has been used. Reroll if necessary. Place the scone on a baking sheet prepared with parchment paper. Brush the egg wash over the scones. Bake the scones for approximately 15-20 minutes, or until they are golden brown.

Serve warm.

Bread Pudding with Whiskey Caramel Sauce

My Grandma Barb would always make bread pudding with raisins growing up. So much a staple in my childhood that I find it hard to pass up the simple delicacy on a menu. Done right, the pudding melts in your mouth. The whiskey caramel adds that bit of depth that pairs so well with the warming nature of cinnamon, a delectable play of complimenting flavors that reverberates comfort all the way through.

4 cups soft bread, cubed
2 ½ cups milk, heated
¼ cup unsalted butter, melted
⅓ cup coconut sugar
4 eggs, slightly beaten
½ teaspoon sea salt
1 teaspoon cinnamon
¼ teaspoon ground nutmeg
¼ teaspoon ground clove
⅓ cup seedless raisins

Whiskey Sauce
¼ cup unsalted butter
¼ cup brown sugar
¼ cup heavy whipping cream
2 tablespoons whiskey
Pinch sea salt

Directions
Preheat the oven to 350°F.

In a large mixing bowl, combine the bread, sea salt, cinnamon, nutmeg, clove, and raisin. Set aside.

On the stovetop, heat the milk to just below boiling. Melt the butter in the milk and dissolve the sugar in the mixture. Remove from the heat. In another medium bowl, crack the eggs and whisk lightly. Temper the eggs by pouring a slow stream of milk into the eggs while continuing to whisk. Continue until the entire milk mixture has been incorporated into the eggs. Pour the liquid over the bread and gently stir until all the ingredients are evenly combined. Transfer this mixture to a 1 ½ quart baking dish and place this dish in a pan of hot water 1-inch deep. Bake for approximately 40-45 minutes, or when a knife is inserted an inch from the edge comes out clean.

While the bread pudding is baking, melt the butter and sugar together in a small saucepan. Whisk in the cream and bring the sauce to a simmer. Continue to cook the sauce for two minutes, constantly whisking. Add the whiskey and whisk for 30 seconds before removing the sauce from the heat. Stir in a pinch of salt and let cool until serving.

France | Chocolates & Champagne
Memories Made in Meaningful Moments

From Mont Sant Michelle, a pilgrimage that topped my bucket list, to sitting on a café terrace not but steps from the Louvre serving the most mouthwatering Quiche Lorraine, France never disappoints. I spent my 23rd birthday touring the Musee de Orsay and enjoying a charming Parisian dinner solo at a lively local bistro in the Republic Arrondissement.

Every memory I have of France involves food, from a canelé de Bordeaux to Breton oysters or token wine tasting paired with chocolate in Dijon. *The epitome of gastronomy*, France has since 2010, been recognized for its meals and rituals surrounding food as an intangible UNESCO cultural heritage. The extraordinary attention paid to the pleasures of the table are found in everyday life, and if you stay long enough, you too will be engulfed in its gratifications and way of being. Led by example, one can be inspired by the French or Europeans in general for their love and appreciation for good food. One of the many clichés about France is that mealtimes are celebrated, if not considered sacred, with individuals spending hours reveling over long meals with friends or on their own, while Americans are known worldwide for the opposite. A study published by the economic think tank OECD reported the French spend an unhurried two hours, 11 minutes a day drinking and eating, far above the average of one hour 30 minutes. The French spend the most time dining compared to any other country surveyed. Americans came in far below the average, spending the least time eating and drinking at one hour.

Slowing down, you can find the most inexplicable pleasure in one of the simplest acts of life, dining. The gastronomic meal stresses togetherness, the joy of taste, remembrance, and the balance between human beings and the products of nature. There is so much meaning that if we step foot out of the hamster wheel of modern life, we become vested in seeing and experiencing it in a different manner.

Challenge yourself to step outside your comfort zone, become aware of where you might be living life on autopilot, and create new habits. Not only can fostering more presence and investing time in cooking and eating be beneficial to your health, but it also boosts your mental wellbeing and connection to your surroundings and the people you do life with. When you recollect a memory from the past, say a holiday meal from childhood, notice what emotions are aroused. Often good memories come to light. Baking cookies with your mother, strolling through a Christmas market tasting local delicacies, or gathering around the table on Christmas Eve with extended family you may not see so often. Holidays and occasions surrounding food give our families tradition and comforts that last our lifetime and beyond. Memories that stay in people's minds are the things done repeatedly as a tradition; they are meaningful and rouse the spirit.

Start a tradition. As a parent, looking back at my childhood, I can recount the good old days when supper was served at 6 pm, and grace was said. Being called in from doing "gymnastics" on the porch rail to help do the dishes or shuck corn and throw the husk over the fence for the cows are daily remembrances. My responsibility is now to embark on old traditions and foster new ones with my two young children.

Garlic Confit

Simply satisfying and a permanent countertop fixture, garlic confit has a similar flavor and texture to roasted garlic, but you don't risk overdoing it by burning it in the oven.

Subtle, rich, sweet garlic taste without the bitter undertones you sometimes get from roasting, garlic confit can be smeared on a piece of toasted baguette or added to your favorite mushroom cream sauce or steak marinade. Don't throw out the cooking oil. Drizzled on a salad with a beautiful balsamic vinegar, my thoughts drift back to days in the restaurant industry. An everyday break with a manager meal, a salad atop an open face quesadilla, the random moments captured in time through taste. Traveling through time, friends and colleagues, weddings and events, and career highlights all flutter back and bring a smile to my face. Allow yourself these connective pleasures. Stroll through the catacombs of our past, revisiting the days that have led you to the here and now.

1 ¼ cups whole garlic cloves, peeled
1 bay leaf
4 sprigs fresh thyme
1 small sprig of fresh rosemary
1 cup olive oil

Directions

Combine the ingredients in a small saucepan and simmer over low heat until the garlic is tender but not browned, about 30 minutes. Let cool

Using a slotted spoon, transfer the garlic and herbs to a small glass pint jar. Pour the oil on top, seal and refrigerate for up to 4 months.

Country Pâté

Not in Paris, but sitting at The Three Staggs public house in London, journaling about the confluence of life in deep reflection (a space I was so often in while travelling solo), I waited for a very French dish in England. Pâté, the French word for paste, is basically just that, a spreadable mixture made out of a wide range of ingredients from mushrooms to chicken. In my rendition of the dish that had brought me back to that corner gastropub whenever I was in London Town. I am not sure if it was for the food or to submerge myself in history at the Imperial War Museum adjacent to this delectable food find, but one thing was for sure, this gem was conveniently located. The nerd in me would be back time and time again.

Food. It not only satiates the hunger, but has the power to make you feel good too. Known for its sustainable, locally sourced fare, the attributes I look for when dining out- I value knowing the foot print I am making is light.

Looking back, relishing the day with a cold pint of lager in hand, and a heaping slice of country pâté, one could indulge in the simplicities of life without rush or dismay.

....

½ pound ground beef
½ pound ground pork
1 cooked smoked chicken breast
16 ounces uncooked chicken livers
Milk
2 tablespoons butter, divided
1 small onion, chopped fine
¼ cup cranberries
¼ cup cognac
2 eggs
¼ teaspoon thyme
¼ teaspoon sage
⅛ teaspoon ground rosemary
¼ teaspoon sea salt
⅛ teaspoon ground black pepper
¼ teaspoon nutmeg
¼ cup parsley, chopped

Directions

In a small bowl, just cover the chicken livers in milk. Set aside for 30 minutes.

Preheat the oven to 350°F. Line the bottom of a 9x5 inch loaf pan with parchment paper and brush the sides with one tablespoon of melted butter.

Melt the second tablespoon of butter over medium-low heat in a small sauté pan. Add onions and cook until tender and slightly browning about 5 minutes. Add cognac and cranberries and cook until no more liquid remains. Turn off the heat and let it cool.

Combine the ground beef, pork, and one egg in a large mixing bowl. Add the seasonings, thyme, sage, rosemary, salt, and pepper. Incorporate the onion mixture and parsley until evenly mixed.

Drain the milk from the chicken livers. In a food processor or blender, combine the chicken breast and liver and puree until smooth.

To assemble, press the ground beef and pork mixture into the prepared loaf pan. Pour the chicken mixture over the top.

Place the loaf pan into a larger baking dish and pour water up two-thirds of the way to the top of the loaf pan. Slowly place the water bath in the oven. Bake for 2 hours, or an internal temperature of 160°F has been reached. Remove and place cardboard wrapped in tin foil over the top of the pate. Add weights, i.e., a bag of dry beans or cans of tomatoes. Allow cooling for 24 hours before serving.

French Onion Soup

A classic in the world of soups, French Onion Soup originated in France in the 18th century and has been a national treasure and an international hit ever since. When it comes to chilly evenings cozied next to the fire, there is nothing more comforting yet somewhat romantic. Heaping spoonfuls of decadent caramelized onions in a rich broth all topped with cheese encrusted croutons is an indulgent affair of sensual proportions.

3 tablespoons olive oil
6 medium yellow onions, sliced
2 cloves garlic
2 bay leaves
4 sprigs thyme
5 allspice berries
2 tablespoons unsalted butter
1 teaspoon coconut sugar
½ cup white wine, to deglaze
2 tablespoons all-purpose flour
1-2 teaspoons sea salt
8 cups beef broth, low sodium
2 beef bouillon cubes, to taste
2 tablespoons brandy or whiskey, optional
French baguette, sliced on a diagonal
2-cups Gruyere cheese, shredded

Directions

Heat the olive oil in a large pot over medium-low heat. Add the onions, garlic, bay leaves, thyme, and allspice berries and cook until the onions are very soft and caramelized, about 25-30 minutes.

Add the butter and sugar and continue to cook over medium-low heat until browned. Add the wine, bring to a boil, reduce the heat, and simmer until the wine has evaporated, approximately 5 minutes. Discard the bay leaves, thyme, and allspice berries.

Sprinkle the onions with the flour and stir. Turn the heat down to medium-low so the flour doesn't burn, and cook for 10 minutes. This eliminates the taste of raw flour. Add the beef broth and beef bouillon cubes, bring the soup back to a simmer and cook for 25 minutes—season to taste with salt and black pepper.

To serve, preheat the broiler. Arrange the French baguette slices on a baking sheet covered with parchment paper. Sprinkle the shredded Gruyere cheese over the sliced baguette and broil until bubbly and golden brown, 3 to 5 minutes. Ladle the soup in bowls and nestle several of the Gruyere croutons on top.

Quiche Lorraine

A French signature dish, the Quiche Lorraine is comprised of a flaky buttery crust that holds the most velvet custard of eggs, lardons, and nutty gruyere. An absolute delight. Served any time of day with a fresh green salad lightly dressed. Sip a glass of Chablis and be mesmerized by the moment-by-moment details making up the wholeness of one's life experience.

Years ago, I watched Rick Steves, the travel writer and PBS television host known for his adventure guides across Europe, talking about Café Le Nemours. A delectable find steps away from the Louvre. Classically furnished with the quintessential sidewalk terrace, the space, the hum of cars and scooters zipping by locals conversing in French, and watching the pedestrians pass, you feel like you are a part of the heart and soul of the city having a truly French experience. While I have found the French culture is not always inviting (of course, there are exceptions), it is moments like these, the ones you carve out and take note of where you feel completely immersed and a part of the greater whole. Vive la France!

1 ½ cup all-purpose flour
8 tablespoons cold butter, cubed
⅓ cup cold water
¼ teaspoon sea salt
1 teaspoon butter
1 shallot
12 ounces lardons, cured pork belly, cubed
8 eggs
¼ teaspoon nutmeg
½ cup whole milk
½ cup cream
½ teaspoon sea salt
¼ teaspoon ground black pepper
2 cups gruyere cheese

Directions
Preheat the oven to 350°F.

In a food processor, combine the flour, butter, and salt and pulse until pea-sized crumbs form. Slowly add the cold water until a firm ball of dough forms. Remove to a floured surface and roll out to a 12-inch circle, large enough to cover a 9-inch pie or tart pan. Cut the excess dough hanging over the edge, leaving just enough to crimp the crust if desired.

In a medium sauté pan, melt the butter and sauté the shallots over medium heat until transparent. Add the lardons to warm. Remove from heat.

In a large mixing bowl, crack the eggs and whisk in the cream, milk, and seasoning until well combined.

Layer alternating the lardons and cheese into the prepared quiche crust. Slowly pour the egg mixture over the top and transfer it to the oven. Bake for 45-55 minutes or until the egg custard is just baked through. The crust will be nicely browned. Let stand for 15 minutes before slicing to serve.

Baked Ratatouille

Baked Ratatouille is a harmonious medley of vegetables stewed together in a delicious tomato sauce. Served chopped or sliced, there are many versions of the much-loved dish made more popular by Pixar's famous movie. Do you want to get your kids to fall in love with their vegetables? Sit for movie night then invite them into the kitchen to get their hands in on the fun. I guarantee it will be an activity they will remember.

2 zucchinis, sliced thin
1 eggplant, sliced thin
1 yellow squash, sliced thin
3 tablespoons olive oil
1 small onion, minced
3 garlic cloves, minced
2 Hot House tomatoes, deseeded, finely chopped
½ cup roasted red bell pepper, chopped
1 teaspoon dried thyme
1 teaspoon dried marjoram
1 bay leaf
¾ teaspoon sea salt
Cracked black pepper to taste
2 tablespoons basil, chiffonade

Directions

Preheat the oven to 375ºF. Slice all the vegetables. For the eggplant, place the slices face up on a plate and lightly salt. Set aside while you prepare the sauce.

In a large sauté pan, heat the olive oil over medium heat. Add the onion and garlic and sauté until tender. Add the finely diced tomatoes and roasted bell pepper and bring to a gentle simmer—season with thyme, marjoram, bay leaf, sea salt, and cracked black pepper. Simmer over medium-low heat for 8-10 minutes before adding a chiffonade of basil. Remove from heat.

In a round baking dish ladle 2/3rds of the sauce into the bottom. Pat dry the eggplant removing any excess salt. Arrange the vegetables, alternating colors in a circular pattern. Spoon the remaining sauce ornately around the center of the dish.

Cover with tin foil and bake for 35 minutes. Remove the foil and continue to bake for another 20 minutes until the vegetables are tender. Serve warm.

Coquille St. Jacques Scallops Au Gratin

The façades and towering ramparts of St. Malo rising from the fortifications give the town its breath-taking silhouette. Situated on the North Coast in Brittany, the restaurants in St. Malo boast some of the best seafood. A true gourmand when it comes to dining, I am picky and don't want to stumble into a tourist trap, leaving me less than impressed. Being the most visited town in Brittany, that was the fear. Canvassing menus displayed at restaurant entrances, I remember meandering the streets of St. Malo with an inpatient partner in tow, making the best-educated decision. Leaving a lasting memory, not only with the heated exchange of words as my indecisiveness finally waned and a restaurant was chosen, but how the temperament changed when at last, the most exquisite meal was enjoyed.

1 shallot, minced
1 clove garlic, minced
2 tablespoons unsalted butter
2 tablespoons flour
⅓ cup white wine
½ cup milk
1 lemon juiced
¾ cup Emmental or Swiss cheese, shredded
1 cup fresh bay scallops
2 cups fresh jumbo scallops

Mashed Potatoes:
3 cups potatoes, peeled
3 tablespoons Greek Yogurt
Sea salt and pepper, to taste

Bread Crumb Topping:
¼ cup Emmental or Swiss cheese, shredded
¼ cup breadcrumbs
1 tablespoon fresh parsley, chopped

Directions

Preheat the oven to 425°F.

Boil the potatoes until tender. Drain the water and add the Greek yogurt. Mash the potatoes into a smooth consistency and season with salt and pepper. Spoon the potatoes into a pastry piping bag and set them aside.

Stir together the breadcrumbs, Emmental cheese, and fresh parsley in a small bowl.

In a large sauté pan, melt the butter. Add the onion and garlic and sauté over medium heat for 2 minutes. Whisk in the flour and cook for one minute. Continue to pour in the liquids, wine, milk, and lemon juice, whisking as you do. The sauce should thicken quickly. Add the cheese and whisk to combine. Turn off the heat and dry the bay scallops before adding them to the sauce.

In 4 individual baking dishes, arrange the jumbo scallops. Pour the sauce over the scallops, evenly distributing it over the four dishes. Pipe the edge of each dish with the potatoes and sprinkle the bread crumb mixture in the center.

Bake for 15 minutes or until the breadcrumbs start to golden. Serve warm.

Aubergines à la Bonifacienne
Eggplant Bonifacio

Bonifacio, the most picturesque town on the French island of Corsica in the Mediterranean, is magnificently situated on a limestone promontory off the southern coast. We were sailing for two weeks, and everywhere you looked, restaurants offered aubergines à la Bonifacienne. The local way to prepare eggplant had my curiosity perked. An interesting technique, boiling the eggplant, the flesh spooned out and blended with milk-soaked bread, eggs, garlic, basil, and sheep's cheese, the mixture is then stuffed back into the skin and fried in olive oil on both sides. My version is lighter, as I roasted the eggplant before scooping the insides out and baked the final dish in the oven instead. As with many traditional recipes, the origin of this dish is to use up leftover bread and cheese. A delectable vegetarian main, especially if you find a smoked sheep's cheese. Alternatively, you can also use a pecorino, ricotta salata, or Parmigiano Reggiano.

2 eggplants
Sea salt
4 cups of ciabatta bread cubed
Milk to cover the bread
2 eggs
2 cloves garlic
2 tablespoons basil
Pinch ground black pepper
2 cups smoked sheep cheese or regular
sheep cheese, grated

Directions
Preheat the oven to 425°F. Line a baking sheet with parchment paper.

Cube the ciabatta bread and place it in a shallow bowl. Just cover with milk and set aside.

Clean and halve the eggplants. Sprinkle salt over the four halves and let rest for 30 minutes or until beads of sweat form on the flesh of the eggplant. Pat dry with a paper towel. Place flesh side down on the parchment paper. Bake for 30 minutes and allow to cool slightly before scooping out the innards into a food processor. Keep the remaining skin of the eggplant ready to be filled.

Strain the bread from the milk, squeezing out any excess and discarding it. Place the bread, eggs, garlic, basil, a pinch of pepper, and 1 ½ cup of the sheep cheese into the food processor with the roasted eggplant. Process until combined. Scoop the mixture back into the eggplant skins. Sprinkle the remaining cheese over the eggplant. Bake at 375°F for 25-30 minutes or until the cheese is golden brown. Serve warm.

Duck à l'Orange

While I have travelled extensively through France, not all my best French food memories were made there. Duck à l'orange is one such case. In London, a culinary rival to Paris, you can find every cuisine under the sun and some of the best in fact. Food is subjective. Restaurants and chefs can have a bad night, but when you find a gem, stay loyal.

Done right, duck a l'orange is incredible; crunchy skin with exceptionally juicy meat countered by a semi-sweet orange sauce. Done wrong, you'll end up eating chewy skin, tough, dry meat masked in an overly sweet sauce.

My hopes are that you will find this recipe falls under the latter category and has you coming back for more.

Duck:
1 apple, chopped
1 red onion, chopped
4 mandarin oranges, segmented
Bunch parsley
2 Bay leaf
6-pound duck, cleaned, with innards, wingtips, and excess fat removed

Butter for coating:
2 tablespoons butter
½ teaspoon thyme
½ teaspoon marjoram
½ teaspoon sea salt

Coating liquid:
1 cup vegetable stock
3 tablespoons honey

Orange sauce:
2 tablespoons sugar
1 garlic clove, minced
4 oranges, zested and juiced
⅓ cup red wine
¼ cup Grand Marnier or you can substitute a quality whiskey
1 bay leaf
2 whole allspice
3 tablespoons unsalted butter
Salt and pepper to taste

Directions
Preheat the oven to 350ºF.

In a small roasting pan, stuff the duck with a piece of apple, onion, and mandarin oranges, placing any extras around the duck in the pan. Coat the duck with the butter mixture of thyme, marjoram, salt, and pepper. Place in the oven to cook for 2- 2 ½ hours. Using a pastry brush, coat the duck with the honied vegetable stock every 20-25 minutes.

While the duck is cooking, begin the sauce. Add 2 tablespoons of sugar to a small saucepan and caramelize over medium-low heat. As it starts to lightly brown, whisk in the garlic, 1 tablespoon of orange zest and fresh orange juice. Cook for 5 minutes over medium-high heat, beginning to reduce the mixture. Add red wine, Grand Marnier, bay leaf and 2 whole allspice berries. Continue to cook over medium heat for 15-20 minutes. Add butter and season with salt and pepper. Set aside.

When the duck has reached an internal temperature of 165ºF, remove it from the oven. Pour the pan drippings into the sauce and reheat while you carve the duck. Serve the duck with sauce spooned atop the meat.

Pork Cassoulet
Pork Casserole

Much like chili on a cold winter's night, pork cassoulet has the same warming effect. A hearty comfort food, one can't go wrong with crusty bread to lather up all the goodness. Simple ingredients that are accessible and won't break the pocketbook, this dish is easy to make and feels like a familiar hug.

One caveat—you must love pork

3 tablespoons olive oil
1 pound ground pork
½ pound lardons (cured pork belly, chopped)
½ pound Canadian bacon, chopped
4 cloves garlic, minced
2 medium onions, sliced thinly lengthwise
2 carrots, sliced
3 vine ripe tomatoes, seeds removed, diced
1 (15-ounce) can tomato puree
4 cups chicken stock
1 (15-ounce) can cannellini beans, drained
1 (15-ounce) can kidney beans, drained
2 teaspoons dried thyme
1 teaspoon dried rosemary
1 ½ teaspoon sea salt
½ teaspoon ground black pepper
1 cup unseasoned breadcrumbs
2 tablespoons fresh parsley, chopped fine

Directions
Preheat the oven to 400ºF.

Heat the olive oil over medium-high heat in a large, enameled cast iron pot. Add the onions and garlic and sauté for 2-3 minutes, until fragrant. Add the carrots and continue to cook for 2 more minutes. Start to brown the ground pork without completely cooking it. Add the pork belly lardons and Canadian bacon. Stir in the diced tomatoes and puree. Season with dried thyme, rosemary, salt, and pepper. Pour in the stock and bring the mixture to a simmer for 25-30 minutes.

While the pot is simmering, chop the parsley and combine it with the breadcrumbs in a small bowl and set aside. Gently fold in the beans. Before placing the dish in the oven, spread the breadcrumbs over the top. Bake for 1 hour uncovered. Remove and let stand 5-10 minutes before serving.

Le Pain des Morts
Bread of the Dead

A specialty of Bonifacio, named Le pain des Morts, means Bread of the Dead. A brioche with raisins and walnuts, this bread had us coming back for more. Moored in Bonifacio's marina for the night, we stumbled upon a small bakery where we bought a warm loaf with our coffee. So entranced by the almost rum-like flavor, we devoured the first round on the spot. Thankfully there were four of us to share the guilt as we divvied up a second and unabashedly bought a third for the boat.

1 ½ cup bread flour
1 package baker's yeast
¼ cup butter, melted
¼ cup sugar
2 eggs, plus 1 yolk
½ cup of milk, warmed
⅓ cup raisins
⅓ cup walnuts
1 lemon zest

Directions

Pour in the flour, sugar, melted butter, eggs, milk, zest, and yeast in a bowl. Mix gently at first and then more energetically.

Flour your work surface, place the dough on it and knead for about ten minutes. Chop the nuts, add the raisins, work the dough folding in the ingredients to combine, and make a ball. Flour it, then cover with a clean cloth and let it rest for about 1 hour at room temperature. The dough should typically rise thanks to the yeast. Take it out of the bowl and cut it in half. Brush both with egg yolk.

Preheat your oven to 350°F. Place a sheet of parchment paper on a baking tray. Place the two loaves so that they do not touch each other even if they rise during baking. Bake for 40 minutes. To check that the Pain des Morts are ready, insert a blade of a knife into the center on the bottom of the loaf. If it comes out clean and the top of the bread is golden, it means the bread is ready. Enjoy immediately or slice, toast, and slather with butter.

Financiers
Small Almond Cake

Sitting at an outdoor café at the base of the South Mountains in Phoenix, Arizona, one might not have expected to find exquisite French baking. Guided solely by reviews, my friend Lily, her dog Honey, and I gave it try. Falling in love with their warm almond muffin served with a seasonal jam, Morning Glory Café quickly became a fan favorite. Like scones, I am sucker for homemade treats. And a further draw, this treasure of a find catered to our four-legged friend much like you would experience on a terrace in France.

10 tablespoons unsalted butter
¼ cup whole wheat flour
1 ¼ cup almond flour
⅛ teaspoon sea salt
⅓ cup powdered sugar
5 egg whites
½ teaspoon vanilla extract
½ teaspoon almond extract
1 tablespoon shaved almonds, optional

Directions

Preheat the oven to 325ºF . Prepare muffin tin or financier pan by coating the edges with a thin layer of butter, then coat with flour. Set aside.

In a small sauté pan, melt the butter until froth forms. Continue to cook over medium to low heat for about 8-10 minutes until the butter has browned, and you will see some solids form on the bottom of the pan. Stir on occasion and remove from the heat when done.

While the butter is browning, combine the whole wheat flour, almond flour, and salt in a medium-sized mixing bowl. In a separate bowl, whisk the eggs whites together until light and frothy. Add the powdered sugar to the egg whites slowly as you continue to whisk. Continue with the vanilla and almond extract.

Pour butter into the dry ingredients and begin to mix. Slowly fold in the egg whites. Using an ice cream scoop, spoon batter into the prepared tins. Optional- Decorate batter with shaved almonds. Bake for 20 minutes or until lightly golden. Using a paring knife, loosen the muffins from the tin and lift them out to serve.

Served simply on their own or with a delicious strawberry jam.

Cherry Galette
Rustic Cherry "Pie"

Many renditions of this French version of what some might consider an "American pie" exist, but my favorite tends to be cherry. And why you may ask when peach, blueberry, apple, or strawberries could grace the table. While it may take extra work, pitting fresh cherries in season, the result is well worth the effort. Having spent extensive time in Poland during the summer, I have been spoiled by the fresh fruits one can find. So often, I can be caught sitting with a bowl of cherries or raspberries, eating one vibrant jewel until the whole lot is devoured. With an abundant market close by or farmers stand on the street corner, there is always a quick top-up within reach. A galette is a rustic catch-all term for a pastry base with just the right amount of sweetness and flaky buttery crust. While I prefer a fruit-filling, savory fillings like tomatoes, caramelized onions, or courgette (zucchini) can all be roughly folded in to create a unique, gorgeous, mouthwatering bake.

1 ½ cup spelt flour or whole wheat
1 teaspoon sugar
¼ teaspoon sea salt
1 stick cold butter, cubed
⅓ cup ice water
1 egg white

Filling:
2 cups fresh cherries, pits removed
½ orange, juiced
½ teaspoon cinnamon
1 teaspoon fresh ginger, minced
2 teaspoons brown sugar
Pinch sea salt

Directions

Preheat the oven to 375°F. Line a baking sheet with parchment paper and set it aside.

In a small mixing bowl, combine cherries, orange juice, cinnamon, ginger, brown sugar, and sea salt. Mix until combined and set aside.

Combine flour, sugar, salt, and cold butter using a food processor. Pulse until small pea-sized balls form and remove the mixture, pouring it into a medium mixing bowl. A pastry cutter could also be used here. Add the water. Pulse until a dough ball starts to form. Press the ball into a round disc and wrap in cellophane. Chill in the refrigerator for 2 hours, or you can use it right away. This step will not change the outcome significantly.

Using a floured surface, roll out the dough into a circle about 1/4 inch thick. To transition the dough to the parchment-lined baking sheet, fold the circle in half and in half again, creating a wedge. Lift the dough from the floured surface, gently placing it on the baking sheet, and unfold. Pour the cherry mixture into the center, leaving about 1 1/2-inch border of dough. Fold this portion of the dough inward, enveloping the filling, but not covering it completely. Note: Work quickly as you want to trap all the juices in. The dough will not be uniform, giving it a rustic, homemade look. Taking a pastry brush, brush the egg white over the dough, giving it a soft sheen. Bake in the oven for 40-45 minutes until the crust is a golden brown and done on the bottom.

Belgium | Liquid Bread
Mountains & Valleys, Memories are Made through the Highs and Lows

Belgium was never on my radar as a destination I would call home, but after one night in Bruges spent on a bar crawl with strangers who are now friends, my life would take a new course that would chart a new chapter.

In a land that often gets overlooked and misconstrued as part of Germany or France, Belgium is a country where everyone can find their place. A melting pot of cultures, especially the capital Brussels, the mix is a beautiful tapestry of human existence.

It is easy to be overwhelmed by what is different, so much that we close ourselves off to experience, but that is not where life should be lived. Instead, when faced with diversity, challenges, and strife, we should foster curiosity and wonderment about what could be. This is across the spectrum, not only with food, delving into a new cuisine like Ethiopian (one of my favorites, by the way), where eating with your hands and serving the first bite to your neighbor is customary, but it should be a common practice when meeting a stranger on the street or engaging in a new profession or trade.

As a society, we are quick to judge one another or compare ourselves to an enhanced image on Instagram. We say no to change, hoping to stay within our comfort zone out of fear of the unknown. We limit our own growth and stay within the parameters of a conditioned mindset. We so often forget that life is lived through the ups and downs, the discomfort and joy. That to feel happiness, one must also experience sorrow. Progress is found when we embrace the disparity, the learning curve from yesterday to today and onward to what life holds in store for us tomorrow.

When I first moved to Belgium, I had no guarantees I could stay. It was a complete gamble. Having sold all my things back in the United States, I rolled the dice and bought a one-way ticket to Brussels, where those friends I met in Bruges would help me lay the foundation of a new beginning. Uncertainty, not one's friend, can show up as that voice of the unconscious telling you that you made the wrong decision and that you're failing. The dark angel on your shoulder tells you why life won't work out, but if you can brush them aside, you'll realize that while unknowing is hard, it's not forever. I did the inner work to make the outer work come to fruition. I wasn't confident what the outcome would be, but I knew if I knocked on enough doors, one would finally open.

Uncertainty eventually waned, and I landed a position as a lead yoga instructor and project manager at a luxury spa. Essentially, I was hired to open a wellness studio and grow their community. Through the highs and lows of the experience that got me to this point, I leaned on the tribe that welcomed me in like family. The group of individuals, despite our varying backgrounds and journeys, opened their arms and homes to me.

Having moved to Belgium in the heart of winter in January 2013, I was confronted by self-doubt right from the outset. Still, I found my way past my own dubious devices through the kindness of others who didn't even know me.

My very first dinner on the night I arrived was foretelling. I was invited to an intimate gathering of friends. Vegetarian at the time, the host, Dave, was flustered and apologetic when I declined the steak he served. Assuring him that no offense was taken, we laughed the night away.

Warm-hearted and congenial, my coterie took me in and helped me find my way. So much that I applied for my visa in Krainnem, one of the Dutch-speaking suburbs of Brussels, and my Flemish friend Liza and her dad, a member of the senate, helped progress the paperwork that allowed me to stay. My dreams became a reality, dawning a new day.

As a yoga and meditation instructor, I often lead a self-care meditation that asks students to visualize a holiday getaway to Italy or Greece—a weekend discovering a place, indulging their interests, and feeding their passions. I ask students if they had one day to spend in Florence or Santorini, what they would do, and then picture going out and doing just that. Upon returning to their boutique lodging in this meditation, the owner has invited all the guests on the property to dine together. Under the stars, seated at one long table, individuals enjoy a coursed dinner and intellectual conversation. People from all over the world join in breaking bread and overcoming barriers to listen, speak, engage, and understand. When we foster curiosity, we open ourselves up to learning, to surprise, and the chance opportunity that might lead to a new beginning.

Belgian Endive and Pear Salad
with Walnuts and Bleu Cheese

Catering the launch of the Poperinge edition of the Belgian Beer and Food Magazine at the Renaissance Brussels Hotel, I served up boats of endive salad. This beautiful bitter-leafed vegetable is not popularized enough in the U.S. Still, it is readily consumed in Belgium, so much that for this event, in partnership with Bookalokal, I nearly ran out of food. If you know me, I like to plan and try to circumnavigate any hiccups. With esteemed figures in attendance, we made sure there was plenty of beer, and the conversations flowed.

3 medium heads Belgian endive
1 Anjou pear, sliced thin
¼ cup gorgonzola cheese
1 stalk green onion, sliced
¼ cup black walnuts

Dressing:
3 tablespoon olive oil
½ lemon, juiced
1 tablespoon apple cider vinegar
1 teaspoon honey
1 teaspoon Dijon mustard
Pinch sea salt and pepper

Directions

Prepare all the salad ingredients for plating. In a small mason jar, combine the dressing ingredients. Close the lid tightly and shake to combine.

Arrange the endive, layering the leaves with slices of pear fanned in portions. Crumble the gorgonzola cheese over the top and evenly disperse the walnuts and onion. Drizzle the prepared dressing over top and serve.

Tomates aux Crevettes
Shrimp Stuffed Tomatoes

A man I met in a posh Belgian nightclub swept me away. Oohing and aahing me, my not yet husband at the time took me on a road trip to the Belgian seaside long before I entertained the thought of forever. The week after I had visited my aunt for the last time, this was a nice way to divert my thoughts of loss. Discovering the sandy beaches of Oostende, Belgium's summer holiday destination along the English Channel, this day in February was cold, gray, and windy. Not so uncharacteristic of a Belgian winter, the weather did not hamper the experience.

Tucking into a seaside café for lunch, Bartosz was keen on introducing me to his favorite Belgian dish. Though, not oft to admit the positives about living in Belgium, on this day, he was out to impress, and that he did. Grey shrimp, also known as 'Purus', is genuinely a Flemish delicacy, the "caviar of the North Sea." With a more pronounced taste than the traditional larger, pink shrimps, combined with in-season Belgian tomatoes and lettuce with homemade mayonnaise, what more could you wish for. With a glass of white wine in hand, my aunt would have wished me that moment and the many moments to come. You can always find light in the darkest of days if you are willing to see it.

4 tomatoes on the vine, poached, remove skin
2 cups North Sea Shrimp or Salad Shrimp, cooked
1 egg yolk
½ cup walnut oil
1-2 teaspoons strong mustard
½ lemon, juiced
1 teaspoon fresh parsley, finely chopped
2 teaspoons fresh dill, finely chopped
Salt and pepper to taste

Directions
Whip the egg yolk and mustard together with an immersion whisk or medium bowl and traditional whisk. Slowly drizzle oil in while firmly whisking the egg yolk. Gradually the mixture will thicken and become slightly glossy. When all the oil is combined, spoon in the mustard, and squeeze in the juice of half a lemon. This will make the mayo even lighter in color. Stir in the parsley and the dill and season with salt and pepper. Combine the herbed mayo with the shrimp and set it aside.

On the stovetop, bring a pot of water to a boil. Make a small cross incision into the bottom of each tomato. Once the water is boiling, gently place each tomato in the water for 15-30 seconds or until the skin slightly starts to pull away from the flesh. Remove the tomatoes from the water and carefully peel away the skin. Using a paring knife, clean the inside of the tomato of seeds. Take a pinch of salt and season the inside of each tomato. Spoon the shrimp mixture into the tomato until full. Let chill before serving.

Chicken Waterzooi
Chicken Stew from Flanders

A country that boasts three national languages, French, Flemish, and German, one can also expect the cuisine to have the same cultural influences. Waterzooi, literally meaning "boiling water", is a must have chicken stew that is emblematic of Belgium. Visiting Ghent, a bustling university town and cultural hub halfway between Brussels and Bruges, with my father I was set on showing him the best of Belgium. From World War I tours in Ypres (Leper) and a truly French dinner experienced near the border, I felt that a more traditional Flemish affair should be had in one of Belgium's most architecturally rich and epicure destinations.

Belgium often splits into regions, Flanders to the North, Wallonia to the south, and the Brussels Capital Region, are very different politically, culturally, and linguistically but make up the melting pot that is Belgium. Embracing the differences, one might find that this juxtaposition makes the country all the more unique and some may say fascinating.

1 medium onion, minced
2 cloves garlic, minced
2 carrots, peeled, sliced thin
2 stalks celery, diced
1 leek, sliced
2 chicken breasts, cubed small
4 cups chicken broth, low sodium, divided
2 bay leaves
3-4 sprigs fresh thyme
¾ cup cream
2 tablespoons cornstarch
1 egg yolk
1 ¼ teaspoon sea salt
Cracked black pepper to taste
Bunch of parsley, roughly chopped for garnish

Directions

Melt the butter in a large pot over medium heat. Cook the onion, garlic, leeks, carrots, and celery, frequently stirring, for about 10 minutes, until softened. Add enough broth, about 2 cups, to just cover the vegetables and bring to a boil with the bay leaves and fresh thyme. Add the chicken and cover the pot. Cook for about 10 minutes until the chicken is cooked through.

Whisk together the cream, cornstarch, and egg yolk in a small bowl. Whisk the cream mixture into the vegetables. Add more broth to thin as desired, constantly stirring to combine.

Season with salt and pepper and bring to a low simmer. Cook for 2 to 3 more minutes until heated through and remove the bay leaves and thyme.

Divide the soup among bowls and garnish with chopped parsley.

Stoemp
Vegetable Stuffed Mashed Potatoes

Spending most of my time in Brussels and the Flemish region, there is no wonder I have a fondness for stoemp. Much like other recipes in this cookbook where you can make your adaptations or use leftover ingredients, the same can be done here. Have leftover carrots or mushrooms? Not sure what to do with the sauteed spinach in the restaurant takeaway container?

Stoemp is your answer. It is that comfort food that can be a meal or served as a side. Rainy days, much like the weather on the British Isle, are plenty in Belgium. Nothing is more satisfying than a warm shawl, hot cup of tea, and a bowl of stoemp to keep the spirits high and energy lifted.

2 tablespoons unsalted butter
4 medium yellow potatoes, washed and cubed
1 leek, sliced
1 carrot, peeled and diced small
½ small onion, minced
1 cup broccoli florets, small pieces
½ cup chicken stock, low sodium
½ cup white wine
½ cup cream
1 teaspoon sea salt
¼ teaspoon nutmeg
Cracked black pepper to taste

Directions

Peel and cube the potatoes. In a large pot, boil the potatoes. When tender, drain and mash.

In a separate sauté pan, melt the butter. Add the onions, leek, carrot, and broccoli and sauté over medium heat for 5 minutes. Add the white wine and continue to cook for another 3 minutes cooking out the alcohol. Pour in the chicken stock and cream and season with salt, pepper, and nutmeg. Cook on a low simmer for 10 minutes.

When the vegetables are cooked, strain liquid out of vegetables and reserve. Add about 2/3rds of the vegetables into the potatoes. And mash with a handheld potato masher. Stir in the remaining vegetables. Add reserved liquid back into the pan. Reheat to a low boil and cook the sauce, stirring continuously, until the sauce reduces and becomes thicker. Stir into the mashed mixture or spoon over top the potatoes to finish.

Chicken and Mushroom Vol au Vent
Baked Puff Pastry Shell filled with Chicken and Mushrooms

Not ready to say goodbye to the Belgian capital, this was the "last supper" so to say. I had traveled across Europe for close to five months, and it was time to make my way home and figure out the next chapter of my life. It was the end of the summer in 2012, and my friend Lize and I were celebrating our birthdays that were only a day apart. Indulging in a day at the spa, we dined at the bistro on the property, and the Chicken and Mushroom Vol au Vent came highly recommended. With our friend Adrian, we were encapsulated in the moment, discussing the "next steps" for all of us in conversation.
As Robert Frost notes, you come to a fork in the road, and that one decision can make all the difference.

Filling
2 chicken breasts cut in small cubes
1 ½ pints button mushrooms, sliced
2 tablespoons olive oil
1 tablespoon unsalted butter
1 cloves garlic, minced
½ onion, chopped
1 celery stalk, chopped
1 carrot, chopped
½ teaspoon crushed black pepper
1 teaspoon dried thyme
½ teaspoon marjoram
¼ teaspoon ground sage salt to taste
1 tablespoon unsalted butter
2 tablespoons all-purpose flour
1 cup chicken stock
1 cup heavy cream
1 egg yolk

Puff Pastry Cases
2 premade puff pastry packages
1 egg, beaten
2 round cookie cutters, one slightly smaller than the other

Directions
Heat 2 tablespoons of olive oil with one tablespoon of butter over medium-high heat in a large pot. Add the chicken, seasoning it with a pinch of salt and ground black pepper. When cooked through, remove the chicken from the pan and set it aside.

Add the olive oil and butter to the same pan and sauté the mushrooms until brown. Add the garlic, onion, celery, and carrot and cook until no longer raw.

Stir in the spices. Melt 1 additional tablespoon of butter into the vegetable mixture and dust with 2 tablespoons of flour, cooking it until no raw flour is visible. Add the chicken stock and watch it thicken. Pour in the chicken and continue to stir.

In a small bowl, whisk together the heavy cream and egg yolk and slowly pour this mix into the pot. Keep mixing as the cream will thicken.

Turn off the heat and set it aside to cool.

Unfold two prepared puff pastry sheets and cut rounds out of them. Place these rounds evenly distanced apart on a baking tray lined with parchment paper. These are the bases of the vol au vent shells.

Continue to cut some more rounds of the same size, and by using a slightly smaller cutter, cut out the inner portion, so you are left with an outer ring. If you have 10 bases, you need 20 outer rings. And 2 outer rings for each puff pastry base.

Brush the bottom base with egg wash, and place one outer ring on the edges. Prick the middle of the base 2-3 times to prevent that area from puffing up. Then brush some egg wash and place the second ring. Give a final brush of egg wash and repeat for all rounds.

Refrigerate these pastries for 15 minutes.

Bake in a preheated oven at 400°F for 15 minutes or until golden and puffy.
Take them out and spoon the chicken and mushroom filling inside for service.

Boulets à la Liégeoise
Belgian Meatballs in a Sweet and Savory Brown Gravy

I grew up with Swedish meatballs, and to this day, it is a request both my brother and I make of our mother when we visit. A blend of sweet and savory, the rich decadence of the sauce is always alluring. That must be why each pleasurable bite of Boulets à la Liegeoise reminds me of yesteryear. When at a young age, I can remember my great-aunt Darlene grinding the pork in a turn crank grinder attached to the countertop. While not all facets of my childhood have been fond, the moments that surround food were almost always sweet.

For the Meatballs
1 pound grass-fed ground beef
1 pound ground pork
½ cup breadcrumbs
1 yellow onion diced
2 cloves garlic, minced
1 bunch Italian parsley, finely chopped
2 large eggs
Salt and pepper, to taste
Flour for dredging
2 tablespoons olive oil

For the Sauce
2 tablespoons unsalted butter
1 large onion, sliced lengthwise
2 tablespoons coconut sugar
2 tablespoons flour
1 teaspoon dried thyme
1 teaspoon dried marjoram
1 tablespoon red wine vinegar
⅓ cup apple butter
⅓ cup plum butter
3 cups beef stock
2 bay leaves
3-4 sprigs fresh thyme
Sea salt and pepper, to taste

Directions
Mix the beef and pork in a large bowl. Add the breadcrumbs, eggs, parsley, onions, and garlic. Mix thoroughly with your hands and form meatballs, about 1/3 cup each, and dredge in the flour.

Heat olive oil in a large skillet over medium heat. Add the meatballs and brown on all sides, about 3 to 4 minutes on each side. Remove meatballs and set them aside on a plate.

Melt 2 tablespoons of butter in the same skillet. Add the sliced onions and reduce heat to medium-low. Cook until the onions are caramelized. Add the coconut sugar, thyme, and marjoram and stir, cooking for one more minute. Whisk in the flour. Stir in the apple butter, plum butter, and vinegar. Pour in the beef stock and add the bay leaves. Bring to a gentle boil, reduce the heat, and simmer for 20 minutes. Add the meatballs back into the sauce and cook for 15 minutes to heat through. Serve immediately with French fries or mashed potatoes and Belgian beer or wine.

Moule Frites
Mussels and Fries

I could hear the rumble of a tram shuttling down the track as I sat on a café terrace with friends I had made volunteering at an English language camp in Genk in 2013. Catching up on life after a summer canvassing the map of Europe trying to find myself, I felt life had come full circle. I had relocated from Phoenix to Brussels and had settled into my job. Living out my dreams, after a shaky couple of years, I finally came into my own. In Belgium I found my tribe, the people I could call family and a place I could call "home". And nothing could be more iconic than to celebrate eating the national dish of Belgium, mussels and fries.

2 tablespoons unsalted butter
2 cloves garlic, minced
1 stalk celery, finely chopped
3 green onions, sliced
1 lemon, juiced
½ cup dry white wine
4-5 sprigs fresh thyme
1-pound fresh mussels

Directions
In a large sauté pan, melt the butter over medium heat. Add the garlic, celery, and green onions. Sauté for 2-3 minutes, and add the juice of one lemon, dry white wine, and mussels. Cook over medium-high heat for 4-5 minutes allowing the mussels to open. Discard any unopened mussels and serve immediately with a crusty baguette and French fries.

Liege Waffle
Waffle with Pearls of Sugar

The aroma can transcend time and space. Down alleyways, through metro tunnels, the smell of yeast and caramelized sugar dancing in the air, enticing your senses and luring you in. The Liege waffle filled with pearls of sugar needs no topping or addition. Perfect on an evening stroll, meandering through the Grand Place, or sitting on a park bench near the Petit Sablon, sometimes we must treat ourselves. Relish in life's little pleasures.

1 packet (1/4 oz) dry rapid-rise yeast
¾ cup warm milk (100°F)
2 cups whole wheat flour
1 ¼ cup all-purpose flour
¼ cup packed brown sugar
1 teaspoon salt
2 large eggs, room temperature
2 teaspoons vanilla
2 sticks (1 cup) unsalted butter
¼ teaspoon nutmeg
¼ teaspoon cinnamon
1 cup Belgian pearl sugar

Directions
Dissolve yeast in warm milk and set aside until a bubbly foam has formed.

Combine flour, salt, cinnamon, and nutmeg in a large mixing bowl. In a separate bowl, cream together the butter and brown sugar. Whip in the eggs and vanilla. Combine the butter mixture and yeast and pour over the dry ingredient; stir until a soft dough forms. Cover and let rise until double in size, 30-60 minutes in a warm, dry place.

Stir in the pearl sugar until evenly distributed. Using a medium-size cookie scooper, evenly divide the dough into small portions. Shape into patties or small discs and arrange on a parchment-lined cookie sheet. Cover and allow to proof for 15 minutes.

Bake in a preheated waffle iron for 3-4 minutes or until a deep golden brown is achieved.

Flourless Chocolate Torte

I had only started dating my husband a few weeks before Valentine's Day in 2014. From the start, he was an utter gentleman. Strengthening the notion chivalry is not dead, Bartek knew I was partial to public transport, but insisted that carrying a chocolate torte from the tram stop to my client's doorstep in the rain was not my best idea. He dropped me off, only to return with a dozen long stem roses.

12 tablespoons unsalted butter
12 ounces (340g) dark chocolate
6 whole eggs
⅛ teaspoon sea salt
½ cup of granulated sugar
Zest of 1 orange
2 tablespoons cocoa powder

Directions

Preheat the oven to 350°F. Butter a 9-inch springform pan.

In a medium saucepan, heat 1 cup of water to a rolling boil. Place a metal or glass bowl over the top, ensuring the bottom does not touch the water. Combine the butter and chopped dark chocolate in this double boiler and stir until melted. Remove from heat and allow to cool for 2-3 minutes.

In a separate bowl, combine the eggs, sugar, and salt. Add the orange zest if you like. Whisk together until light for approximately 5 minutes. Slowly in a steady stream, begin to pour the chocolate into the egg mixture, whisking the entire time not to curdle the eggs. Pour the batter into the springform pan. Bake in the oven for 35-40 minutes or until the top is no longer shiny; the cake may still wiggle slightly. Remove and allow to cool entirely before removing it from the pan.

Dust the cake with cocoa powder and serve.

Spain | The Quintessential Siesta
Stories Lock our Treasures in a Trove

Stepping foot in Plaza de la Constitucion, a historical square in San Sebastian, you notice the numbers above each window on the houses facing inward. These numbers are a historic mark once identifying the bullring boxes that the houses formerly used to be and from which you could watch the bullfight. In 2009, on a solo venture across Europe, I had spent my 23rd birthday in Paris, made my way south through Bordeaux, and crossed the border where most pilgrims start their journey on the El Camino de Santiago and found myself dining on pintxos in this famed courtyard in San Sebastian buzzing with life. Never would I have thought that day sipping a glass of verdejo and savoring the freshest catch, a grilled squid with smoked black sea salt appetizer, I would one day live and work in this beautiful country. Taking in the cool sea breezes, this culinary enclave gives Barcelona a dueling partner for the acclaimed title of a culinary capital. Maybe they both deserve to tout the honor.

Fast forward to the end of 2014, Bartek and I were married after dating eight months, and relocated to Barcelona. A thriving Mediterranean port city just south of the Costa Brava, Barcelona is an expat's dream. With over 10,000 restaurants, of which 20 are Michelin-star, a history rooted in Roman conquest and medieval heritage still visible in the Gothic quarter today, world-class art museums and galleries such as the Picasso, the Miro or the MNAC, the scenic Eixample with its Parisian-looking art-nouveau architecture, and the Gaudi works, there is so much to see and do. A memory makers wonderland, you could spend years peeling away the layers, meshing tradition with modernism.

The stories are tied up in a chapter that has since been read. Looking back, I may not have been privy to all the beauty that surrounded me at the time. At the moment, we are hardly ever that conscious of how unique our lives are in an instant until we look back in the rearview mirror or find ourselves recounting tales to another.

This wisdom should remind us to live now—experience every taste, smell, texture, and beautiful plate. Open yourself up to chance encounters and new affairs. Nothing is off-limits. Ask yourself. What will be the story you tell your grandkids, the fellas over coffee, or the hairdresser fancying your fading locks when you get to the end of your days?

During our time in Spain, we traveled. To Madrid, south to Murcia, back through Valencia, up the Costa Brava, into Girona, La Garotxa, La Rioja, Figures, to the border into the Pyrenes, across to Mallorca, and back up to Andorra. Every mode of transportation exhausted-we only scratched the surface. You can't do it all in a country steeped in history, sports, and culture. From exploring the wine regions celebrating my 30th birthday at

Vivanco and the Museum of Wine Culture to visiting Figueres and Cadaqués, the birthplace of Salvador Dali and his residence. We bundled up in freezing temperatures to watch FC Barcelona and get an expansive view from Vallter 2000, a ski resort near the French border. Everywhere we discovered regional delicacies and wines straight from the source. If there was only one place I could retire, it might be in Spain.

The stories, and more so now the memories, are like reels of film meant to be consumed and serve as a reminder that there is so much still to be lived. Travel, flirt with possibility, get caught up in a language you can't entirely comprehend, take a wrong turn, wander, get lost, or sit for dinner with strangers; life will meet you right where you are meant to be.

Coca Mallorquina
Pan de coca & Pan con Tomate

Passeig de Sant Juan, a central avenue in Barcelona connecting Gràcia and a part of the Eixample neighborhood with the Arc del Triomf, is well known for its little local eateries like El Viti Taberna that beckon passersby to sit on their outdoor terraces. A cozy bricked-lined restaurant around the corner from our first flat on Consell de Cent was a lovely central place to meet for drinks or a coffee with friends. Barcelona has many gems tucked in every nook, but not all are alike. El Viti Taberna stands out because the bar serves the best pan con tomato on coca bread in my opinion. An incredibly popular dish in Barcelona, the bread makes all the difference. Light and airy, toasted and rubbed with garlic and vine-ripened tomato, the pan con tomate is finished with a pinch of flaked salt. Sometimes keeping it simple is perfect.

3 cup bread flour
2 cups water
1 tablespoon water
1 teaspoon dry active yeast
½ teaspoon sugar
1 ¾ teaspoon sea salt
2 tablespoons olive oil

To make the Pan con Tomate

Good quality olive oil
Whole garlic cloves
Campari tomatoes
Flaked sea salt
Cracked black pepper

Directions

In a bowl, stir the flour with the water and mix until a uniform mixture is obtained. This can also be done in a standing mixer with a paddle attachment. We knead with the help of the hook, or you can do the process by hand, which I prefer.

Mix until no flour remains. Cover this mixture with a film and make autolysis for 1 hour and 40 minutes. During this time, dissolve the active dry yeast into 1 tablespoon of water, salt, and sugar. Once the time has passed, incorporate the yeast mixture into the flour mixture and mix again.

Transfer the dough to a clean work surface and begin kneading, doing the French kneading technique. Quite a bit of additional bread flour will be used here as the bread is quite sticky and moist. Alternate 3-4 minutes of kneading with 5 minutes of rest until the dough acquires strength, muscle, and a smooth exterior surface.

Once we have the dough at this point, add the oil. Ideally, pour little by little and knead the dough simultaneously to add flavor that integrates well. Make sure the dough has developed gluten well before bulk fermentation.

Grease a large Tupperware with olive oil and put the dough inside. Place the cover on tight and let stand for 1 hour and 30 minutes at 75° F folding the dough over once every 30 minutes. In total, three folds will be made, and, after making the last one, keep the dough in the cold until the next day 12-15 hours.

Remove the dough from the fridge and let it stand for 15 minutes at room temperature. You will get a dough that has quadrupled in volume and has a surface full of bubbles.

Prepare a large wood cutting board, cover with baking paper and sprinkle with flour. Set aside.

Generously sprinkle a work surface with flour and turn the dough over. If necessary, help the dough slide from the container and avoid tearing it. It is very, very important correct the shape of the dough so as not to damage the internal structure of gaseous bubbles. Stretch the dough gently to shape a rectangle.

Using a metal scraper, divide the dough into two equal pieces. Sprinkle the surface with flour, cover with a cotton cloth, and stand for 45 minutes at room temperature.

Preheat the oven to 480°F and place a small baking dish filled with water on the bottom shelf of the oven. Preheat the oven with it inside. Also, place the baking sheet the bread will bake on in from the beginning. Ensure there is enough water to create steam for the first round of baking at the highest temperature. Let oven come up to temp.

When the oven is ready, slide the bread with the wood board's help or lift the parchment paper, gently transferring the dough to the very hot baking sheet. Bake for 5 minutes with the steam. After this time, remove the water and reduce the oven temperature to 465°F and continue to bake for 10 minutes.

Lower the heat to 445°F and bake 5 more minutes. Take the bread loaves out of the oven and let them cool completely on a rack.

To make the Pan con Tomate

Directions

Preheat the oven to 425°F. Line a baking sheet with parchment paper.

Slice the pan de coca down the middle and again slice these pieces into 2-inch segments. Drizzle with a good quality olive oil or use a pastry brush to apply the oil. Bake the bread until it starts to become golden brown. Remove the bread from the oven and while it is still warm, take a clove of garlic and slice it widthwise. It's okay if the peel is still on. Rub each piece of bread with the garlic. Next, slice your Campari tomatoes in half. Rub a tomato half onto the toasted side of the bread. The tomato flesh will remain on the toast as you work until the peel is all that is left in your hand. Top with flaked salt and a crack of black pepper.

Mediterranean Inspired Baked Eggplant
with aged Manchego Cheese

A mashup of memories, this spice blend recipe was passed down from a friend to a friend and is an amalgamation of the most unique flavors. From juniper berries and yellow curry to fennel seed and smoked paprika, the portions seem small, but the bold taste and aroma are catching. Balanced by the smooth rich flavor of a good quality Manchego, the savory combination is pure magic. While I adore the eggplant chips drizzled with honey you can find in many tapas restaurants in Barcelona, I find this appetizer is a bit heartier and pairs better with tempranillo, one of the most popular regional red wines.

Spice Mix
2 tablespoons sea salt
1 tablespoon fennel seed
1 teaspoon whole black peppercorns
1 teaspoon whole white peppercorns
1 teaspoon dried oregano
½ teaspoon dried thyme
½ teaspoon yellow curry powder
½ tablespoon juniper berries
¼ teaspoon yellow mustard powder
¼ teaspoon Laurier
¼ teaspoon smoked Spanish paprika

Other Ingredients
1 eggplant, sliced thin, skin on
Manchego cheese, sliced

Directions
Preheat the oven to 425ºF.

In a coffee grinder or spice mill, combine all the spice mix ingredients and grind until a fine powder is created.

Slice the eggplant ½ centimeter thick. Place on a baking sheet lined with parchment paper. Season each slice of eggplant with a large pinch of the spice blend. Bake for 10-15 minutes. Remove from the oven and add the pieces of Manchego cheese to each eggplant and put back into the oven for 5 minutes or until the cheese starts to bubble and brown slightly.

Serve warm.

Escalivada

Always drawing a queue of locals and tourists, Cervecería Catalana is considered one of the best places to try a tasty assortment of tapas in Barcelona. Whether hosting friends or hitting the bar after a show for a few light bites, we are creatures of habit ordering our favorites first, with a few specials thrown in. A decadent round of goat cheese warmed with flambéed sugar set atop a beautiful blend of roasted vegetables that play well with each other; escalivada always tops my list. Thinking about it makes me salivate and calculate the probability of our next trip.

2 red bell peppers
2 Chinese eggplant
2 small onions, unpeeled
2 tablespoons olive oil
1 clove garlic confit, mashed
Salt and pepper to taste
1 small round of goat cheese
1 teaspoon sugar

Directions

Preheat the oven to 450ºF. Line a baking sheet with parchment paper and lay the vegetables atop. Brush the peppers and eggplant with olive oil. Bake the vegetable for 30 minutes. The bell peppers and eggplant will be tender and have blackened skin, remove. Leave the onion to cook another 10 minutes.

Place the peppers in a Ziplock bag and allow them to cool. This will help easily peel away the skin, remove the seeds, and slice them into thin strips. Continue to do the same with the eggplant; remove the skin and gently remove the seeds, and place the vegetables into a bowl. The eggplant will naturally flake apart. Finally, trim away the onion peel and slice lengthwise. Toss the mashed garlic clove into the mix and salt and pepper to taste. Allow resting for at least 1 hour or overnight to allow the flavors to blend.

Use a round mold and spoon the eggplant mixture into the center of a plate to serve. Press down with a spoon and remove the mold. Top the form with a thin round of natural goat cheese. Sprinkle the sugar over the top. Using a small torch, caramelize the sugar. Serve with toasted bread as an appetizer, a tapa, or a side dish with a meal.

Melon Gazpacho

From May until October, you can find Spain's grocery stores and fresh air markets stocked with beautifully ripe watermelon, juicy sweet cantaloupe, and the most popular melon grown in Spain, the Piel de Sapo, among others. Eaten as a snack, pureed into a smoothie, or as a salad with lunch, you could find a way to eat melon for every meal without tire. A refreshing raw soup that is sweet and savory, melon gazpacho is undoubtedly one of my favorite go-to "treats" - light, healthy, and utterly satisfying on a sultry sunny day.

3 cups melon, rind and seeds removed, chopped
1 large beefsteak tomato, remove seeds, chopped
1 medium cucumber, peeled, sliced
1 red bell pepper, remove seeds, chopped
½ white onion
¼ cup olive oil
3 tablespoons red wine vinegar
½ teaspoon dried cumin
½ teaspoon smoked paprika
Salt and pepper to taste

Directions
Purée melon, tomato, cucumber, bell pepper, onion, oil, and vinegar in a blender until smooth. Add in the spices and pulse to combine.

Prepare Ahead: Gazpacho can be made 1 day ahead. Keep chilled.

Top with a drizzle of olive oil or a chili-infused oil, crumbled feta, and/or a chiffonade of mint.

Tortilla Española
(Sweet) Potato Omelet

A favorite of home cooks and tapas bars in Spain, tortilla española (or tortilla de patatas) is a tender omelet made traditionally with white potatoes, but for this rendition, I wanted to give it a healthy spin. Sweet potatoes provide color, caramel-like sweetness, and are also loaded with beta carotene, which functions as a potent antioxidant and a rich source of vitamin A. I like it when foods work for me.

3 tablespoons olive oil
3 sweet potatoes, peeled and sliced thin
1 small onion, sliced thin, lengthwise
10 eggs
2 tablespoons cream
1 teaspoon sea salt
Large pinch of black pepper
½ teaspoon dried parsley
½ teaspoon dried oregano

Directions
Preheat the oven to 425°F.

In a large oven-safe sauté pan, heat the olive oil and cook the onion and sweet potatoes covered over medium to medium-high heat for 10 minutes. Stirring from time to time to make sure the potatoes are evenly cooked. During this time, whisk together the eggs, cream, salt, pepper, parsley, and oregano in a large bowl. Pour the egg mixture into the sauté pan, moving the potatoes around to make sure to evenly distribute the potatoes within the eggs and assure that the eggs reach the bottom of the pan, cooking for 2 minutes.

Turn off the stove and transfer the sauté pan into the oven to bake for 15 minutes until set. Remove the pan from the oven and let cool slightly before inverting it onto a serving dish to serve.

Pulpo a la Galega
Pieces of Octopus over Boiled Potatoes

When we lived in Spain, whenever we went out for tapas, this dish was ordered. Tender bits of octopus drizzled with olive oil and dusted with paprika. Simple right? The boiled potatoes provide bulk to the dish, making it more filling, adding textural contrast and mild background flavor. My husband loves it, and when it is prepared right, still tender, and moist, I can go fork to fork with my man. That is the key here—the preparation. Pulpo a la Galega is something special because it is not every night you partake in a plate, unless you are in Spain, in which you could binge to your heart's content.

1 pound octopus (fresh or defrosted from frozen)
4 quarts water
3 teaspoons sea salt
2 bay leaves
Olive oil
Smoked & sweet paprika
Lemon, juiced, optional garnish
3 large yellow potatoes, peeled and cubed

Directions
Fill a large stockpot with 4 quarts of water and bring it to a boil. Add the sea salt and bay leaves. Once boiling, rapidly dip the defrosted octopus three times into the boiling water, dunking the octopus for 15 seconds and removing him for 15 seconds each time. Finally, place the octopus into the water (making sure it's fully submerged) and cook for 12 minutes per pound on a low boil. Adjust the cooking time based on the weight of your octopus.

Remove the octopus from the heat and let it rest on a plate or cutting board for 15 minutes. Once cooled, slice the tentacles, and serve with high-quality olive oil and a sprinkle of paprika (I like to use both sweet and smoked), sea salt, and lemon (if desired). Serve over lightly salted boiled potatoes.

Pollo Catalana
Chicken with Prunes and Raisins

I suppose you have noticed a pattern; the sweet and savory combination is the butter to my toast. This dish is no exception. Using a whole chicken, don't throw the carcass into the bin. This is not only something we are taught in culinary school, but I put it into practice in Barcelona, where we entertained and regularly cooked at home. If you want to invite friends over, this dish will impress but double up. Depending on appetites, one whole bird may not be enough.

1 whole roaster chicken fabricated into individual pieces
2 tablespoons olive oil
2 medium onions, sliced thinly lengthwise
3 cloves garlic, minced
¼ cup cognac or whiskey
1 cup white wine
1 cup chicken stock
1 15-ounce can stewed tomatoes
1 bay leaf
3-4 sprigs fresh thyme
1 cinnamon stick
2 tablespoons pine nuts
20 prunes
⅓ cup raisins
¾ teaspoon sea salt
⅛ teaspoon ground pepper

Directions
In a large skillet, heat the olive oil over medium heat. Add the onions and garlic and sauté until tender. Add the cognac, white wine, chicken stock, and stewed tomatoes. Using a wooden spoon, break up the tomatoes into smaller pieces—season with bay leaf, thyme, cinnamon stick, salt, and pepper. Add the prunes and raisins and simmer uncovered for 15-20 minutes, reducing the liquid. Place the chicken pieces into the sauce and spoon the liquid over the top. Cover and continue to cook for 15-20 minutes or until the chicken is cooked. Serve with brown rice or egg noodles.

Bacalao a la Baezana
Cod Filet with Vegetables

Bacalao (cod) is a mainstay in Barcelona and on tapas menus across the country. I never really got into salt cod, though you could find this in every grocery store.

Serve this as an appetizer or as a main dish, and you will dazzle the night. Accessible ingredients, the trick is to find a good quality wild-caught filet of cod.

Fabricate it into the portion sizes that suit your needs, and do not overcook it. The fish should taste buttery and light.

While I never jumped on the paella bandwagon, I could easily eat Bacalao a la Baezana after a long summer's day at the beach.

4 filets of wild-caught cod (approx. 8 oz each filet)
¼ cup all-purpose flour
3 tablespoons olive oil
½ onion, chopped fine
2 cloves garlic, minced
¼ cup almond slivers, toasted
3 Roma tomatoes, diced small
⅓ cup roasted red bell pepper, chopped fine
½ cup frozen peas
1 cup vegetable stock
¾ teaspoon sweet smoked paprika
1 bay leaf
¼ teaspoon ground coriander
Sea salt
Fresh ground black pepper
2 tablespoons parsley, chopped fine

Directions
Pat dry four cod filets and season with salt and pepper on both sides. Add ¼ cup of all-purpose flour to a large plate and evenly coat the fillets in flour.

In a large frying pan over medium heat, dry roast the almond slivers and remove from heat. Set aside. Wipe the pan clean and pour 3 tablespoons of olive oil in. Heat over medium-high heat. Add cod filets and cook on each side for three minutes. Remove filets from the pan and let rest on a plate covered with a paper towel. Leave browned bits in the pan and add the onions and garlic. Sauté until aromatic and translucent. Add tomatoes and bell pepper and cook for 2 minutes. Add half of the almonds, vegetable stock, smoked paprika, bay leaf, and ground coriander to the pan and simmer until reduced by half. Add the frozen peas and cook until thawed. Do not overcook.

Add salt and pepper to taste and return the cod fillets to the sauce. Heat the cod for 1-2 minutes, remove the pan from the stove and serve with freshly chopped parsley.

Panellets

Panellets are a seasonal sweet in Catalonia, offered only for a short period leading up to All Saints Day (November 1), where they are traditionally served alongside roasted chestnuts and enormous roasted sweet potatoes. Bought at a local panadería or from a vendor at the market, many autumn favorites can be savored at a café or on the street. Homemade or store-bought panellets often thought to be of Arab origin are celebratory and often paired with a sweet wine.

1 ½ cup pine nuts (alternatives: sesame seeds or almond slivers)
3 eggs, divided
2 small yellow potatoes, cooked and mashed
⅓ cup brown sugar
⅓ cup powder sugar
1 lemon, zested
3 cups almond flour

Directions

Prepare the pine nuts or alternatives the day before. Crack two eggs and whisk them together with the pine nuts or alternative. Let set in the refrigerator overnight.

Bake the potatoes until tender, peel, and let cool. In a large bowl, mash the peeled potatoes. Add the sugars, lemon zest, and remaining egg. Gradually add in the almond flour and stir the dough until it is thoroughly combined, taking care not to overwork it. Using a cookie scoop or spoons, scoop out equal amounts of dough, rolling it into balls about 1 ½ inch thick. Preheat the oven to 425°F. Ready a baking sheet with parchment paper.

Using the pine nut washed in eggs, gently start conforming the nuts to the balls. Be patient here, as it may take a bit of finesse to get the nuts to stick. Place the balls 1-inch apart. Bake for 10-minutes or until the tops of the panellets turn golden brown. Be sure to watch closely as they can burn quickly. Remove when done and let cool.

Sangria

While the term sangria has been around since the Roman times, it was on a food tour of Barcelona that two cheeky Spaniard guides were mixing up their recipe for a group of thirsty twenty-some's regaling us in a tale of its origin. In their rendition of sangria's beginning, they said there was a delegation of Spaniards that had attended a world's fair in France back in the 18th century. The Spaniards were impressed by seeing the French muddle together fruit with wine. Spaniards being Spaniards in their sly ways, took the recipe from the French and hid it in their back pocket, and claimed sangria to be their own making. While I may not do the story justice, the group was rolling in laughter, sitting in a restaurant known for its paella and strong drinks. It also didn't hurt the two male guides wore butterfly aprons all the while. Don't forget to have fun and laugh when recalling life's colorful moments.

1 apple, cored and chopped
1 orange, halved and thinly sliced
½ cup sliced strawberries
1 (750 mL) bottle Tempranillo or Grenache red wine
⅓ cup Cointreau
⅓ cup good quality brandy
½ cup orange juice
½ cup Fanta

Directions
Place the apple, orange, and strawberries in a large pitcher. Pour in the wine, Cointreau, brandy, orange juice, and Fanta, and stir. Chill overnight to allow the fruit and wine to infuse one another. Add more orange juice or Fanta if you like a sweeter drink.

Serve in glasses filled with ice.

Poland | New Chapters, A Country Reborn
Document a Life Well Lived, But Don't Outsource Your Memories Entirely

In a world of social media, it is becoming ever more popular to capture moments in time on an app, website, or simply your phone. From telephone numbers to photos, storing our memories on an external device means that we will likely devote little mental space to remembering them. Research published has shown the more we store data or meaningful moments outside our brains, the more improbable it will be to recall that information later. It is like the info commercial "set it and forget it." If our coffee machines can do it, then so can our brain. We snap a photo capturing a moment and move on. It begs the question, if you are not present and aware of the dinner or an event you are attending, will you be able to evoke the feelings and sensations you experienced again if you are distracted taking pictures or writing a caption to a post?

Think about it. Two decades ago, when the sit-down family meals midweek were the norm and cellphones weren't a distraction, we were engaged in conversation and the actual act of eating. We said grace and looked each other in the eye rather than carelessly scrolling a device. Times have changed, but it is up to us how we let outside influences affect our lives.

***

To say I love visiting Poland is an understatement. It feels like my second home. Every Sunday during the summer, my in-laws have an afternoon dinner either right after church or early evening when the heat of the day has faded away. While my husband's immediate family is not large, it is close-knit, which I missed during my adolescence. Encapsulating that feeling of belonging to a nuclear family soothes my inner child and carving out the time to be in their presence is magical.

Teściowa is the word for mother-in-law. Even though my *teściowa* cannot speak English and my Polish is not mastered, we share the common language of food. Rarely one to go to restaurants; my husband says this is a generational byproduct of living through the Cold War. She is adamant about making everything homemade. Dedicated to her family and always ready to host a guest, I awe how she balances it all. Even in her seventies, she still runs a tourism office. When we are visiting, she busies herself in the kitchen from early morning to late at night, making extra meals and snacks to have on the ready in the refrigerator. She knows our favorite dishes and makes them often. Think pierogi, naleśniki, and sałatka jarzynowa among many others.

If you ever get the opportunity to travel to Poland, seize it. The hospitality, the food, the history, and fascinating enough, the architecture will move you. I picked up the book called *Poland*, a historical novel written by James A. Michener and published in 1983, at a second-hand English bookshop in Brussels years ago. It may even have predated my husband. It was such a fascinating read about Poland over eight centuries and how a country entirely wiped off the map for 300 years has been shaped into the land it is today.

Having traveled from the North to the South and back up again, on my own and with my husband, I have fond memories of taking a taxi across the Vistula River in Warsaw to eat at one of my favorites in the city's Praga-Południe neighborhood, Warszawa Wschodnia. Serving up a fusion of French and Polish dishes, this trendsetting restaurant fits the area known for many great food finds and artsy vibes. Heading outside the capital, heading back north towards the sea, we stopped by Restaurant Romantyczna at the Hotel SPA Dr. Irena Eris Wzgórza Dylewskie. Tucked in natural surroundings in a region called Grunwald, this restaurant's chef composes his menu according to the concept of slow food. A prize-winning restaurant we visited early on a weeknight when there were no other guests and had the pleasure of having the chef attend our table himself. Using a smoldering pinecone, he infused a glass with smoke and enclosed beef tartar on a plate, giving the dish a delicate flavor and aroma.

Enticing experiences are not lacking. Poland's eclectic cuisine is full of diversity, but if it were to be described in just one word, "heartfelt" would perhaps be the most appropriate. Its cuisine is one of the most undiscovered gastronomies in the world. In a genuinely resourceful food culture, eating out in Poland is not only highly recommended but also quite reasonable.

Polish cuisine is unpretentious. True comfort food is enjoyable to eat and simply makes you feel good. Nourishing and authentic—it does not try to be exotic or pretend to be something it's not; instead, it utilizes local products and cooking methodologies to elevate its cuisine to a whole new level!

Surówka z Marchewki z Jabłkiem
Carrot Salad with Apples

Quick, simple, accessible, and healthy are words I look for to describe a dish. A typical side in Poland, I love serving this morning, noon, and night. I can't count the number of brunches this dish has appeared at or picnics in the park. Because I have so many memories, I can flip through the photo album on my phone or find it captured on Instagram. The best way to remember is to create it again and again. Keep making memories and loving up on the foods that fill you full, and not only physically. Share recipes that bring you joy, health, and vitality.

5-6 large carrots, grated
1 tablespoon olive oil
2 teaspoons honey
1 lemon, juiced
⅛ teaspoon sea salt
Pinch black pepper
2 tablespoons fresh parsley, finely chopped
1 apple, grated

Directions
In a medium mixing bowl, combine all the ingredients. Stir to combine and adjust the level of sweetness and acidity by adding more or less honey and lemon as desired.

Sałatka Jarzynowa
Vegetable Salad

Made of various vegetables and sometimes apples and hard-boiled eggs, this dish is a staple on the traditional Polish Easter breakfast table and any time of the year. For picnics, birthdays, barbeques, you name it; this recipe is versatile and relatively easy to make in an instant. Having developed my recipe from what I thought my mother-in-law used in hers, I discovered that I was missing a few ingredients. Apples and hard-boiled eggs were unintentionally overlooked, but my husband never knew the difference for the longest time. Only when I was working on this book was she visiting and making the salad for us. While I like her version, I decided to stick with mine. Sometimes recipes get passed down, and they are adapted to the consumer's taste from one hand to another.

3 medium yellow potatoes, peeled, small cubes
1 carrot, peeled, small cubes
1 parsnip, peeled, small cubes
1 stalk celery, small cubes
1 cup sweet peas
1 cup Polish or dill pickles, small dice
⅓ cup mayonnaise
⅓ cup Greek yogurt
2 tablespoons fresh dill, chopped
1 teaspoon fresh parsley, chopped fine
1 tablespoon mild mustard
½ teaspoon salt
Cracked black pepper to taste

Directions
In a large pot, bring the potatoes, carrots, and parsnip to a boil. Cook until tender but not mushy. Remove from heat and drain. Gently fold in the celery, peas, and pickles. Add the mayonnaise, Greek yogurt, dill, parsley, mustard, salt, and pepper and stir until combined. Adjust seasoning to taste. Chill to build flavors overnight.

Śledź w Śmietanie
Herrings in Sour Cream with Apple and Onion

We were on a day trip from Gdańsk to visit a factory that builds brewery tanks. Having been in Poland for three months researching the prospects of buying a hotel that could also house a microbrewery, we were on a cost analysis mission when we detoured off the beaten path through the countryside. Near the seaside town of Darłowo, we found a beautiful farmstead converted into a restaurant and tea house. I was in my element, being served traditional fare on a lace-trimmed table with intricate porcelain. Having met my match, self-professed foodies, Bartosz and I stayed the afternoon tasting, enjoying, and discovering new tastes and flavors of a nation. Herring in sour cream with apple and onion was a dish we ordered at my husband's request. A favorite of his, it has now become one of mine. Served with dense brown bread on this warm summer's day, it was the perfect appetizer. Light and full of flavor this plate epitomizes what I have come to realize in Poland is that sour cream is not just a compliment on a baked potato but a mainstay in the Polish diet. From soups to pierogi, it is lovely as a dressing for fish.

Using a good quality sour cream makes all the difference.

5 Herring fillets, marinated or salted
½ small onion, minced
2 apples, peeled and cubed small
½ cup sour cream
Cracked black pepper to taste
2 spears Polish pickles or pickled
cucumber, chopped small, optional

Directions
Cover the herring filets with water for 2 hours. At the end of this time, discard water and pat dry.

Cut the fillets into small squares 1-inch x 1-inch and place them in a medium mixing bowl. Add the onion, apple, and sour cream. Stir until combined—season with cracked black pepper and taste. The herring are salty, and usually no additional salt is needed. You can add pickles if you like.

Refrigerate overnight to allow the flavors to develop, and serve on dark rye bread or toasted pumpernickel.

Zupa Grzybowa
Cream of Mushroom Soup

It is easy to find dried wild mushrooms at the local grocer in Poland. Even here in Chicago, a city that boasts the largest Polish diaspora outside of Warsaw, you can find these in your big-name chain stores, but for most outside these regional markets, dried wild mushrooms may be hard to come by. For this recipe, while I remember soaking mushrooms that provide the soup with the most profound earthiness, I made do with my preferred mushroom, the shitake. Similar in taste, this soup comes close to my traditional favorite. Want to make it super Polish? Add buckwheat or a spätzle-like noodle to the soup.

It makes it a hearty mainstay, especially comforting in the autumn.

2 tablespoons olive oil
1 medium onion, chopped
1 carrot, chopped
1 stalk celery, chopped
1 clove garlic, minced
1 pint cremini mushrooms, sliced
1 pint shitake mushrooms, sliced
4 ¼ cups water
2 mushroom bouillon cubes
¼ teaspoon ground rosemary
¼ teaspoon ground sage
¾ teaspoon sea salt
Pinch ground black pepper
½ cup sour cream

Directions
In a large pot, sauté the onion, carrot, celery, and garlic in olive oil until fragrant and tender over medium heat. Add the cremini and shitake mushrooms and sauté until they start to brown. Add the water, bouillon cubes, rosemary, sage, salt, and pepper, and bring to a simmer, cooking for 30 minutes. Remove from the heat and, using an immersion blender, puree the soup until smooth. Add the sour cream to combine.

Placuszki z Cukinia
Zucchini Pancakes

I eat a pretty plant-based diet. Becoming more popular in Poland, it is not hard to find vegetarian and vegan friendly foods and restaurants in what some may consider a very meat-focused nation. After Henry was born in Barcelona, he and I quickly moved to Poland for four months while my husband started a new job in the States. After watching What the Health, a documentary emphasizing the link between diet, disease, and the billions of dollars at stake in the healthcare, pharmaceutical, and food industries, my budding family's food habits changed. My husband, a hardcore meat eater and Crossfitter at the time, quit cold turkey and said let's be vegan. I was thrilled as I had been vegetarian for a time before this and was happy to pursue this lifestyle together. When we got to Poland, bless my mother-in-law's heart, she made every accommodation to cook vegetarian. Long story short- these made an appearance on the menu often. Quick and easy to prepare, these zucchini pancakes served with a creamy mushroom sauce, or any condiment really, are versatile and tasty.

2 medium zucchinis, grated and pat dry
2 eggs
¼ cup Greek yogurt
¼ cup all-purpose flour
¼ cup Parmesan cheese
½ teaspoon sea salt
Large crack black pepper
1 teaspoon marjoram
1 green onions, sliced
1 clove garlic, minced
Olive oil, for cooking

Directions

Grate the zucchini into a large mixing bowl. Using paper towels, dab out as much moisture as you can. This step is essential. Too much moisture will cause the pancakes to fall apart.

Add the rest of the ingredients to the bowl and mix until thoroughly combined.

Drizzle a tablespoon of olive oil in a large nonstick sauté pan over medium heat. Spoon approximately two tablespoons of the zucchini pancake mixture into the pan. You should be able to arrange 3-4 pancakes into the pan at a time. Cook until the pancake edges start to appear dry, and flip. Continue to cook the pancakes until golden brown.

Remove from the heat and serve the pancakes warm with a mushroom cream sauce or sour cream.

Pierogi
Spinach and Ricotta Dumplings

When we first started dating, Bartosz had to travel often for work. He was back and forth to Poland while I stayed back in Brussels. On one of his trips back from his hometown of Gdańsk, he brought five takeaway containers with various pierogi for me to taste and enjoy. At least a 13-hour drive, Bartosz sped through Germany, excited to see what I thought of the most recognizable Polish food abroad. I was obsessed, especially with the vegetarian-filled ones, i.e., cabbage and wild mushroom and the spinach and ricotta pierogi. Poles love their pierogi not only out of nostalgia, often reminding adults of childhood and home, but they are also the epitome of comfort, satiating and hearty.

Dough for Pierogi

3 cups all-purpose flour

1 egg

1 cup of warm water

½ teaspoon of salt

4 tablespoons olive oil

Spinach and Ricotta Filling

2 teaspoons olive oil

20-25 oz frozen spinach, thawed

8 cloves garlic

2 cups ricotta cheese

½ cup Parmesan cheese

Sea salt and pepper, to taste

Garnish

Onion

Sour Cream or Greek Yogurt

Directions
Spinach Filling
Heat the olive oil over medium heat. Add the garlic and sauté until aromatic. Add the spinach and cook until warmed, 3-4 minutes. Remove from the heat. Drain or pat the excess water from the spinach with a paper towel. Add the ricotta and parmesan cheeses and stir until evenly combined. Season with salt and pepper and set aside while making the pierogi dough.

Pierogi Dough
Put the flour, egg, oil, and salt into a food processor. Pulse a few times. Add the water slowly, letting it incorporate before adding more. Combine all the ingredients until a large dough ball starts to form. Remove from the processor to a floured work surface.

Divide the dough into 2 or 3 balls. Thinly roll each piece out onto a floured surface to under 1/16 - 1/8" thickness. Use a round cookie cutter, and cut circles from the dough. Spoon the filling (2-3 teaspoons) in the center of each circle. The more filling, the better. However, make sure the filling stays inside the pierogi. Fold the dough over, connect the edge, and seal the dough by pinching the two edges together.

Bring water to a boil in a large pot. Add 2 teaspoons of salt to the boiling water. Gently drop the pierogi in the hot water one by one. When they start floating, wait for one minute and take them out with the slotted spoon.

Serve the pierogis sauteed in onions and olive oil and top with a dollop of sour cream or natural Greek Yogurt.

Łosoś Polski z Jabłkami i Cebula
Salmon with Apples and Onion

This recipe is Christmas. Poland is big on tradition, and when it comes to celebrations, they know how to cater a feast. Christmas Eve or "Wigilia" is the day when the main meal is shared with family. They eat, drink, sing, exchange gifts, wishes, and are merry. The centerpiece of the magical evening is the meal where twelve dishes are served. You might be surprised to discover many of the traditional dishes are healthy and vegetarian. I love spending the holidays in Poland. Unlike the U.S. there is no Thanksgiving to mark the beginning of the season. Instead, St. Nicholas Day on December 6th is when things start to get festive, and the tree only goes up days before Christmas Eve. But don't fret. Decorations typically stay up, casting a joyful light on the new year and throughout the month of January.

2 filets of wild-caught salmon, remove skin
Sea salt and pepper
1 lemon, zest and juiced
2 tablespoons unsalted butter
½ small onion, minced
1 clove garlic, minced
2 honey crisp apples, peeled and cubed small
½ teaspoon fresh thyme, chopped
Sea salt and cracked black pepper to taste
¼ cup dry white wine

Directions
Preheat the oven to 425°F. Season the salmon with salt, pepper, and lemon zest on both sides of each filet. Set aside.

In a large nonstick sauté pan, melt 1 tablespoon of butter over medium heat and sauté the onion, garlic, and apples for approximately 5 minutes or until soft and onions are translucent. Season with fresh thyme, salt, and pepper, and add the wine. Cook until the wine has soaked into the apples and there is no more liquid. Remove the apples to a bowl and set them aside.

Using the same nonstick sauté pan, melt the additional tablespoon of butter and place the salmon filets in searing them for 90 seconds each side. Top the second side of each filet with the apple and onion mixture, juice the lemon over the fish, and transfer the pan to the oven. Bake for 8-10 minutes or until the salmon is cooked to your preferred temperature. Be careful not to overbake the salmon. Serve immediately.

Gołabki
Stuffed Cabbage Rolls in Tomato Sauce

Learning the secret and putting it into practice is satisfying and rewarding when it comes to food. At first, I tried peeling back the layers off a raw cabbage, breaking more cabbage leaves than I cared to, making it nearly impossible to fill. Having asked for and learned the trick, the dish clicked. One of Poland's most popular and well-known dishes, I can finally make it at home with confidence and applause from my biggest fan and sometimes critic, my husband.

1 large cabbage head
2-3 teaspoons sea salt

Sauce
1 24.5 oz jar tomato puree passata
crushed tomatoes
¼ cup heavy cream
Salt and pepper to taste

Filling
2 pounds ground pork or ground
turkey
1 cup white rice, under-cooked (the
rice is still slightly hard or al dente)
1 teaspoon sea salt
¼ teaspoon cracked black pepper
2 tablespoons dried marjoram
½ teaspoon thyme
¼ cup fresh dill, chopped
¼ cup fresh parsley, chopped
2 cups good quality tomato sauce

Directions

Prepare the cabbage by running a knife around the center core. Do not remove the core but loosen the leaves. Place the cabbage head in a large saucepan and fill with water to cover. Season the water with 2-3 teaspoons of salt. Bring to a rolling boil. When the leaves begin to fall away from the core, use a fork to remove them entirely. Make sure the cabbage is tender before removing it. In a colander, shock the cabbage to stop the cooking by running cold water over the leaves.

Preheat the oven to 400°F.

For the filling, precook the rice. In a large mixing bowl combine the uncooked ground pork (or turkey), rice, salt, pepper, marjoram, thyme, dill, and parsley. Set aside until you are ready to assemble.

In a large baking pan, layer leaves of cabbage to cover the bottom. This is used to flavor the sauce and protect the cabbage rolls from sticking to the bottom. Using a large tablespoon, scoop about 1/3 cup of filling into each cabbage leaf. The leaves should be large enough to roll, folding the sides to cover the filling and rolling like a burrito. Place the cabbage rolls tightly into the baking dish, side by side, leaving little room to unroll.

When the cabbage rolls are filled. Top with tomato sauce. Place more lettuce leaves over the top of the sauce to protect the rolls and add flavor to the sauce—Bake for 1 hour.

In a small saucepan over medium heat, bring the tomato puree passata and cream to a simmer. Season with salt and pepper. Set aside for service.

Remove the cabbage rolls from the oven. Spoon the sauce over the rolls' top and sprinkle with fresh herbs to serve.

Kotlety Jajeczne z Brokułami
Ground Meat Patty with Broccoli

It is hard not to rave about my mother-in-law's cooking. She is an all-star in the kitchen, and in line with Polish hospitality, she makes sure there is always plenty of food ready and waiting for famished guests. Now a member of the family, I am left to my own devices when I visit and can open drawers and doors to get what I need or crave without asking. An easy dish to make ahead and in large quantities, I am always guaranteed to see a tray of these patties in the refrigerator. Curious as to why they are so darn delicious, I asked my mother-in-law for her recipe on her last visit to the States, and nothing could make my husband happier. More reminders of home. After his mother flew back across the pond, he was assured he would not go for want of those reminders of his native land.

1 pound ground turkey or ground pork
¼ cup breadcrumbs + 1 cup for bread the patties
1 egg
¼ cup milk
1 teaspoon sea salt
¼ teaspoon ground black pepper
1 teaspoon dried marjoram
2 tablespoons chopped parsley
2 tablespoons chopped dill
½ small onion, minced
½ cup cooked broccoli florets, chopped

Directions

Combine breadcrumbs, eggs, and milk in a large bowl. Allow to set for 2-3 minutes, letting the breadcrumbs absorb the liquid. Add the ground turkey, salt, pepper, marjoram, parsley, dill, onion, and broccoli. Using your hands, mix until all the ingredients are evenly incorporated.

Pour the extra cup of breadcrumbs into a shallow bowl. Form oval-shaped patties about a half-inch thick. Press into the breadcrumbs to coat all sides. Continue with the rest of the turkey.

In a large sauté pan, heat a generous amount of olive oil over medium heat. Place the patties into the pan. Cook for about 8-12 minutes over medium-low heat, flip and continue cooking the patties until cooked through.

Serve with horseradish cream or with a mushroom cream sauce.

Naleśniki
Polish Pancakes or Crêpes

Essentially the Polish version of the French crêpe or the German version of palatschinke. I remember in Home Ec making palatschinke in collaboration with my German language class. There was concern that since we didn't have a crêpe maker the thin pancakes wouldn't turn out, but they did. Plus, anything smeared with jam and Nutella at that age was a win, regardless of their appearance.

Fast forward to the recent past. When I first started dating my husband, his mother would have breakfast prepared and waiting for us on the table. So often than not, a tray of naleśniki would appear accompanied by a spiced plum compote that is my all-time favorite. Inspired by my now mother-in-law and well trained from years of practice, I make naleśniki every other day upon request from my son Henry, my naleśniki junkie. He takes after his mother.

One day, he will take what he has learned at a young age and pass it along.

• •

1 egg
1 cup milk
1 cup water
1 cup all-purpose flour
Pinch sea salt
½ teaspoon honey
1 tablespoon unsalted butter, melted+
butter for coating the pan

Directions
In a large bowl, whisk together all the ingredients until smooth.

Heat a nonstick sauté pan over medium heat. Using a heat-resistant pastry brush, lightly coat the pan in butter. Pour ⅓ cup to ½ cup batter into the sauté pan, and using the turn of the wrist, circle the batter evenly across the bottom. Return to the heat until the edges start to pull away from the sides gently. Flip and cook through approximately a minute more and layer the naleśniki on a plate.

Serve with jam, yogurt, apple puree, nut butter, or a chocolate spread. You name it, naleśniki are versatile. My son will devour ten on their own.

Szarlotka
Polish Apple Pie

The quintessential apple pie in Poland. This recipe is a versatile dessert where the filling can technically change. My mother-in-law has prepared it with macerated plums. On another occasion, when strawberries were in season, she paired them with the bittersweet rhubarb she picked from her garden. This "pie" will be a crowd favorite whether you're a traditionalist or not.

My first memory was sitting in a trendy café on Rainbow Square in Warsaw when Bartek and I were just dating. He had shown me the best eateries and places of note in the capital, from the Warsaw Uprising Museum to Łazienki Park, the Royal Castle to Praga-Południe, a trendy, artsy district full of restaurants, yoga studios, man-made beaches, and of course PGE Narodowy, the national football stadium.

It was my second time in Warsaw after Couchsurfing a few years earlier. The iconic rainbow on the square was still in place, and on that night, we sat under the stars sipping coffee and sharing a tantalizing plate of szarlotka. Whenever I visit my in-laws in Gdansk, this memory fills my heart with the warmth of a person, a family, of a country. So much vested in a simple dessert. That is the true measure of memories.

2 cups all-purpose flour
¾ cup powder sugar
½ teaspoon sea salt
1 teaspoon baking powder
½ cup cold unsalted butter, cubed
3 egg yolks

Apple Filling
6 medium apples
¼ cup water
⅓ cup coconut sugar
½ teaspoon cinnamon
Pinch sea salt

Meringue
3 egg whites
Pinch Sea Salt
2 tablespoons powder sugar

Directions

Preheat the oven to 350°F and lightly grease an 8-inch springform pan with butter, nonstick spray, or line with parchment paper.

Start by cooking the apples in a large pot over medium-high heat with water, 1/4 cup sugar, cinnamon, and a pinch of salt. Bring to a simmer and cook for about 25-30 minutes or until the apples start to fall apart and look soft.

While the apples are cooking, use a food processor to combine the flour, baking powder, salt, and 3/4 cup of confectioner's sugar. Add the butter and pulse until small pea-size crumbs form. Add eggs and pulse until combined, but the dough is still slightly crumbly. Pour 2/3 of the dough mixture into the prepared pan, lightly and evenly distributing it in the bottom. Do not press it firmly down. Place the pan in the oven and bake until puffy and turn golden for about 15 minutes.

Whisk the egg whites with a pinch of salt until light and frothy in a medium bowl. Add the confectioner's sugar and whisk until glossy and stiff peaks form.

Remove the pan from the oven and spread the apples evenly over the top of the cake base. Spoon the meringue over the apples making a thin layer of white. Crumble the remaining cake dough mixture over the meringue.

Return the pan to the oven and bake until the top is golden approximately 40-45 minutes. Let cool completely before serving.

Pavlova
Meringue Dessert

This may be my absolute favorite dessert, and one of the reasons is the fond association it has to summer. A dessert named after a Russian ballerina, Anna Pavlova, has no association with the country but actually originates from New Zealand and Australia. Known for its lightness and various flavor adaptations, this meringue is utterly satisfying, and why not? It is almost purely made of sugar.

A showstopper tantalizes the eye; the pillowing mascarpone in this rendition compliments the meringue's crisp crust and soft inside. Sitting on the seaside at the White Marlin Restaurant in Sopot, Poland, watching the sunset with one of my friends from Zakopane. Summer lingered as the warm night danced, kids frolicked on the white sand beach, and laughter filled the air.

Meringue
6 eggs room temperature
1 ½ cup of sugar
Pinch of salt
½ tablespoon vanilla
½ tablespoon fresh lemon juice
2 ½ teaspoons corn starch

Mascarpone Cream Topping
1-pint heavy whipping cream
½ cup mascarpone
1 ½ tablespoon honey
⅛ teaspoon dried cardamom
Fresh fruits to garnish

Directions
Prepare your granulated sugar. I have found most sugar in the U.S. is too heavy. To curb any over-browning of the meringue, I use a food processor to grind the sugar on high for about one minute. It will not be a powder sugar, but it will not be as dense as before.

Now, preheat the oven to 225° F. Line a large baking sheet with parchment paper. Using your stand mixer or handheld mixer, beat 6 egg whites on high speed for 1 minute until soft peaks form. With the mixer on, gradually add 1 1/2 cups of the prepared sugar and continue to beat the egg whites and sugar for 10 minutes on high speed, or until stiff peaks form that is quite glossy.

Beat in the vanilla and lemon, and gently fold in the 2 ½ teaspoons of corn starch and mix until well combined.

Pipe or spoon the meringue onto the parchment-lined baking sheet into 3 to 3 1/2 inches wide nests. Indent the center with a spoon to allow room for cream. Bake at 225°F for 1 hour and 15 minutes, then turn the oven off. Open the door and place a wooden spoon or another oven-safe utensil to prop the door open. Let the oven cool at least 3-4 hours or overnight, assuring the outsides will be dry and crisp to the tap, very pale cream-colored, and marshmallow-soft on the inside.

Once cool, you can peel them gently from the parchment and top them with whipped mascarpone cream and fruit, or store them in an airtight container for 3-5 days at room temperature in a place with low humidity.

Whipped Mascarpone Cream Topping
Beat cold whipping cream until soft peaks form. Spoon in the mascarpone in three turns, whipping the mixture until the cheese is combined. Add the honey and cardamom and beat until evenly incorporated—pipe or spoon the whipped mascarpone cream onto the pavlova and top with fresh fruit.

Follow Your Taste Buds | Make a Plan and Live in the Present

Take a breath and tune into your senses and surrounding. Don't let life pass you by.

Today, more than ever, there is a need for connection. We have felt isolated and restricted from our normal rhythms throughout the pandemic. With some sense of routine or a new way of life being established, I increasingly yearn to be a part of a community. Gathering around the table to nurture relationships and inspire human connectivity shows us there is still so much to life, even though it might look a little different from before. We can still find reasons to gather, celebrate, set the table, and make moments feel special with our friends and ones we hold dear, even if things have changed.

Let's not take it for granted. For all the silver linings one can find, maybe the slowdown was what we needed to reconnect. A public health crisis opened our eyes and brought many of us back to the kitchen, to the table where it all began. I'm very blessed to have grown up in the 1980s and 90s when dinner or supper was served at 6 o'clock, and life was simple. Paced just right, comfort could be found in just being.

How has life changed since you were little? Think back to your childhood and the fond memories you made around the table. The pleasures of homemade, fresh churned ice cream on your birthday, corned beef gravy on toast at grandma's, or your favorite pizza uptown.

We must be discerning stewards of our lives. The digital age of comparisons, social disconnect, overstimulation, and lack of privacy are not helping us engage fruitfully with one another or find fulfillment every day. Blink, and you'll miss it. Snap a photo, and the moment is gone. Collecting a gazillion images on your phone to catalog the experience is stealing you from the actual experience. Minimize these distractions. Unless you have a plan for these images, no one will ever see them, and the time, what I consider to be our most valuable asset, will have been lost. Nostalgia is the ability to recollect something of value. Our memories are a depository we carry with us that shape us into who we are. Don't let them slip away. Find your system, possibly one that brings you joy, and run with it. Be it a shoebox full of Kodak prints or a scrapbook of recipes with cocktail napkins and wine labels taped inside. Create a cache of wonder that you can reminisce upon and will bring you back to the moment, the taste, the smell, the conversation~ time and time again.

About the Author

Emily Szajda is a writer, chef, yoga/meditation instructor, nutritionist, and avid traveler who left 'Corporate America' managing high-volume restaurants for an entrepreneurial life in Europe. After having launched a successful wellness studio in Brussels, Emily worked with the international recognized Belgian Beer and Food Magazine and catered sumptuous events with Bookalokal. When she isn't in the kitchen or entertaining with friends, she can be found strolling through farmers' markets, playing with her two cherished children in the park, or practicing yoga. Emily has appeared on HGTV's House Hunters International and other multinational media platforms including the Bathtime 2 Boardroom podcast and People on the Grid. Emily resides with her husband and two children, Henry and Olivia, in greater Chicago.

Note from the Author

Word-of-mouth is crucial for any author to succeed. If you enjoyed *Culinary Travels*, please leave a review online—anywhere you are able. Even if it's just a sentence or two. It would make all the difference and would be very much appreciated.

Thanks!
Emily Szajda

We hope you enjoyed reading this title from:

BLACK ROSE
writing™

www.blackrosewriting.com

Subscribe to our mailing list – *The Rosevine* – and receive **FREE** books, daily deals, and stay current with news about upcoming releases and our hottest authors. Scan the QR code below to sign up.

Already a subscriber? Please accept a sincere thank you for being a fan of Black Rose Writing authors.

View other Black Rose Writing titles at www.blackrosewriting.com/books and use promo code **PRINT** to receive a **20% discount** when purchasing.

www.ingramcontent.com/pod-product-compliance
Lightning Source LLC
Chambersburg PA
CBHW040710150426

42811CB00061B/1806